TEA SHOP WALKS
IN
SOUTH DEVON
& DARTMOOR

Norman & June Buckley

Published by Sigma Leisure – an imprint of
Sigma Press, 1 South Oak Lane, Wilmslow, Cheshire SK9 6AR, England.

British Library Cataloguing in Publication Data
A CIP record for this book is available from the British Library.

ISBN: 1-85058-573-3

Typesetting and Design by: Sigma Press, Wilmslow, Cheshire.

Cover: The Gardens at Overbecks, near Salcombe (June C. Buckley)

Maps: Elizabeth Fowler

Photographs: the authors

Printed by: MFP Design & Print

Disclaimer: the information in this book is given in good faith and is believed to be correct at the time of publication. No responsibility is accepted by either the author or publisher for errors or omissions, or for any loss or injury howsoever caused. Only you can judge your own fitness, competence and experience.

Preface

Those already familiar with this popular and fast-growing series will need little or no convincing that South Devon is an absolutely natural choice for the format of combining an attractive but fairly short walk or ramble with the refreshment, in most cases very varied, offered by a teashop.

Many miles of coastline with wonderful scenery and villages, all accessed by the South West Coastal Path, coupled with the huge expanse of Dartmoor and its fringe of superbly attractive river valleys, ensure that there is no lack of walks of the requisite high quality.

On the other side of the equation, the Devon Cream Tea is a national, probably international, institution, provided at a rich variety of traditional tea shops, farm tea rooms and stately homes, probably unequalled elsewhere.

For this book thirty walks, all but one being circular, have been selected with a wide geographical spread across the southern half of the county. From the tranquil surroundings of the Tiverton canal to the wind swept heights of the Moor around Princetown; from the wooded splendour of the Teign valley at Castle Drogo to the wave battered headland of Prawle Point, there is something here for all walking tastes. In assessing walks it has been assumed that footpaths and bridleways are generally preferable to roads, the latter being included only where essential to complete a circuit. Many minor roads do, in fact, have very light traffic and are perfectly acceptable to the majority of walkers. However, every effort has been made to avoid walking along the typical Devon sunken lane, where the high banks, narrow carriageway and twists and turns all contribute to danger for pedestrians.

The summary at the start of each entry is intended to enable a quick decision to be made on the suitability of a walk for any particular occasion, person or persons.

A similar variety has been sought when assessing tea shops to link to each of the walks. It goes without saying that any establishment must satisfy the basic requirements of providing tea and other beverages in pleasant and/or characterful surroundings and offer a welcome to walkers, possibly subject to the removal of muddy boots. Nowadays, the provision of refreshments is generally very flexible and most of the premises included in the book serve varied light meals throughout the day. In addition to the expected tea shops, farms and stately homes, teas can be enjoyed on a canal barge and a former railway platform. As opening times can be changed, sometimes at short notice in inclement weather, telephone numbers are given in addition to the stated hours.

As before in a Tea Shop Walks book, towns, villages and visitor attractions associated with each walk are described and advice is given concerning maps and car parking. South Devon is comparatively well served by public transport and the following information should be useful in respect of many of the walks:

- Devon County Council public transport map - most useful map giving bus service numbers, places served and list of the various operators, with telephone numbers. Not a detailed timetable, although frequency is given.

- "Your summer bus and coach times around Plymouth" - Western National. Comprehensive maps and timetables.

- "Explore Devon and Cornwall by Train" - Devon County Council. Information concerning each railway line and special tickets such as Railrover. Not a timetable.

- "Exe Rail - five lines into Exeter" - Devon County Council. Detailed timetable.

- Railway enquiries. Tel: Plymouth 221300

The above maps and booklets are available at relevant Tourist Information Centres.

Norman & June Buckley

Contents

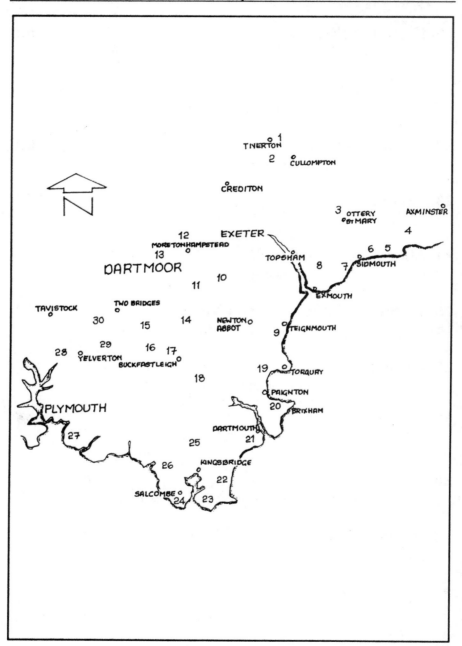

Introduction

South Devon has long been regarded as an area of great character and diversity, with the majority of visitor interest focused on the fine rocky coastline, high cliffs and abundant bird life, beautiful estuaries, sandy beaches and a benign climate permitting the growth of plants which survive in just a few favoured parts of Britain. In short, the "English Riviera" of the holiday brochure.

At least as important in any appreciation of South Devon is Dartmoor, largest and highest of the granite moors of the South West, with its rich history overlaid with centuries of legend and folklore. The eruption of hot lava pushing through the earth's crust has produced the mineral-rich granite, weathered throughout the ages by ice and climatic factors, leaving the profusion of rocky tors which are so characteristic of the Moor.

Human occupation of the area began early, as testified by the finds of hunting implements at Kent's Cavern, Torquay, probably dating from the Palaeolithic or Early Stone Age, 30,000 to 20,000 BC, before the final ice covering had departed from Britain. After the departure of the ice, the land became forest covered and the Mesolithic hunter gatherer people of those times have left the scant evidence of a few flint scatters on Dartmoor. Their successors of the Neolithic, New Stone Age have left a few elevated settlement sites and some burial mounds in South Devon. The finest survivor is the "Spinster's Rock" between Chagford and Drewsteignton. Most importantly, the first cultivation started at this time, with some growth of cereals and the keeping of herds and flocks of domesticated animals.

The following Bronze Age ("Beaker" people) has left much more evidence - barrows, cairns, small stone lined chambers (cists) and, most strikingly, the stone rows of Dartmoor. There are also large numbers of hut circles, the remains of the stone foundations of Bronze Age dwellings, and evidence of a cultivation system high on the Moor, encouraged by the warmer climate at that time. Inevitably, there was large scale clearance of woodland, leading to erosion and the formation of the peat bogs which are now such a feature of high Dartmoor. From the middle ages there has been much looting of the burial sites and also much breaking up and removal of stones from the rows and circles, as a readily available building material. The large earthworks, often known as castles in Devon, date from the succeeding Iron Age.

Also of great importance in contributing to the Dartmoor landscape of today has been the wealth of minerals associated with the formation of the granite. Extraction of the tin by primitive "streaming" started in the 12th. century, much later than in neighbouring Cornwall, leading to the formation by the tin miners of the Stannary Parliament, with real legal powers, meeting for centuries at Crockern Tor. Mining for the ore commenced early in the 16th. century and smelting became the method of extracting the metal from the stone. Many "blowing houses" were constructed and the furnaces were kept intensely hot by the operation of bellows worked by water wheels. Remains of these houses and the associated waterways can still be seen on Dartmoor.

Copper, lead, silver and zinc were also mined, but to a lesser extent than tin. Other industries with significant landscape impact are stone quarrying and the extraction of china clay, the area around Lee Moor on the south edge of Dartmoor almost rivalling St. Austell in Cornwall as a "lunar landscape" Granite from Haytor quarries was used extensively in constructing such prestigious structures as the British Museum, the National Gallery and London Bridge.

The need to transport quantities of bulky, heavy material has left its very distinctive mark on South Devon . Very early railways such as the ten mile long Haytor Granite Tramway used granite blocks as rails and were constructed to a variety of gauges as entirely individual enterprises. Wagons were drawn by large numbers of horses. These tramways or railways were abandoned as soon as their parent industry failed but, in most cases, remains such as blocks of granite can still be found and the line traced.

Equally interesting are the leats which, as early as Drake's time, provided supplies of water from the Moor to the Plymouth and Devonport area. The later Devonport leat still carries water for many miles across Dartmoor.

Not surprisingly, in 1951 Dartmoor was given the status of a National Park, bringing the extra planning protection and ensuring the additional visitor interest and facilities which this outstanding area richly deserves. The total of 365 square miles within the park includes the Moor and most of the fringe area.

The South Devon coast hardly needs further advocacy. Historically, ports such as Plymouth, Dartmouth, Exeter and Kingsbridge have played a major part in creating the seafaring tradition, legendary in Devon since the days of Sir Francis Drake and the Armada. In more recent times visitor popularity has understandably focused on the many and varied holiday resorts. Torquay, Paignton and Brixham have grown to the extent of coalescence into a sizeable conurbation whilst Sidmouth, Seaton, Salcombe and Dartmouth have retained a more individual character. The creation of the South West Coastal Path has opened up the formerly more remote parts of the coast to those prepared to walk.

Between the coast and Dartmoor is a rolling countryside split by the valleys of several of the rivers, now placid, which in their upper reaches have come hustling and bustling down from the Moor. Notable are the Teign, Dart, Avon and Erme. This is an area of interesting old towns, Totnes, Buckfastleigh and Ashburton being particularly rewarding.

In addition to its fine coast, with such a unique landscape feature as the Undercliffe, created by landslips of monumental scale between Seaton and Lyme Regis, the area generally known as East Devon also has good towns such as Ottery St. Mary and Honiton. Quite different from the rest of the area covered by this book is the large area of sandy, heathy common to the east of the estuary of the River Exe, between Woodbury and East Budleigh.

In summation, South Devon is greatly favoured in its wonderful range of natural landscape, overlaid with historic human activities which for the most part have done little to detract from our enjoyment of that landscape. Indeed, the prehistoric remains and the industrial activity of more recent centuries have for many visitors added significant interest to the exploration of the area.

1. Tiverton, Grand Western Canal

Length: 3 miles (extendible)

Summary: An out and back walk along a canal towpath. Entirely level and excellent underfoot. Interesting features along the way.

Car Parking: Informal space for 2 or 3 cars by Manley Bridge, reached by a lane heading south from the Tiverton to Halberton road, opposite Tiverton golf club. Grid reference 987122. For a 5 mile walk park by Crownhill Bridge, reached by a lane leaving the Tiverton to Halberton road a little way to the west of the road bridge over the canal. Grid reference 997128

Map: Ordnance Survey Landranger no. 181, Minehead and Brendon Hills area, 1:50,000.

Tea Shop

The venue selected cannot be called a tea room or tea shop for it is a canal barge on the Grand Western Canal – so there is something quite different here. The barge, which is traditionally decorated in bright colours, is smart, clean and inviting. There are hanging baskets and tubs of flowers everywhere.

Savouries available include sandwiches, filled baguettes, jacket potatoes, bowls of chips, vegetarian options, etc. Cream teas, cakes, ices, milk shakes, tea and coffee. An amazing choice for such a small space and the full menu available throughout the day.

Open 10am – 6pm everyday from Easter to the end of September. Tel – not available

Description

The Grand Western Canal was an ambitious concept whereby Taunton would be linked by water to the English Channel at Topsham near Exeter, with branches to Tiverton, Cullompton and

Wellington. From Taunton other navigable waterways would connect the canal with Bridgewater and Bristol, providing a through route to the Bristol Channel.

Surveys in the 1760s by the great James Brindley, father of canal engineering, were not acted upon and it was not until 1796 that an Act of Parliament was obtained. Again, there were delays and in 1810 the route was re-surveyed by John Rennie and the first 11 miles, from Tiverton to Lowdwells, was constructed, as a level "contour" canal, without locks. The section from Lowdwells to Taunton was started in 1829 and finished nine years later, with the complications of vertical lifts and an inclined plane. However, time was already running out for canals; the Bristol and Exeter Railway was opened in 1844, with a Tiverton branch.in 1848. The grand scheme was abandoned and the relatively unprofitable Taunton section was closed in 1869.

The staple trade was in limestone from Westleigh to Tiverton, with coal to burn the limestone coming from Taunton, by water in

Barge Tea Room, Tiverton

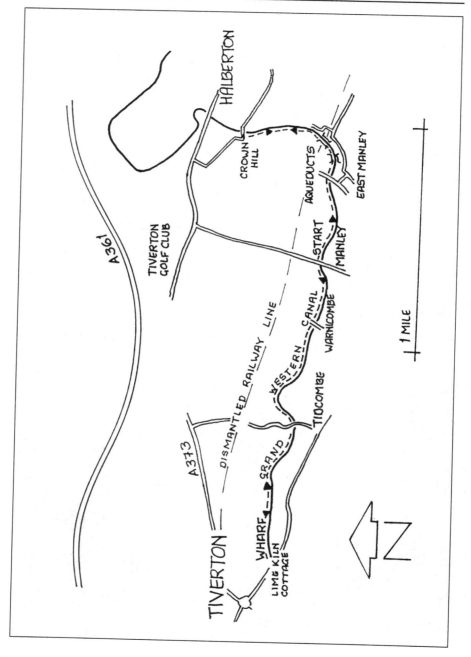

the early years. Eventually, like many others, the canal was taken over by the Great Western Railway and continued to operate in a declining state until a serious leakage in 1924 divided the canal into two parts, virtually ending commercial traffic.

The canal was taken over by Devon County Council in 1971 and is now managed as a linear country park, 11 miles long.

At Tiverton Basin, terminus of the canal, is a fine array of the remains of 10 lime kilns, emphasising the importance of the lime-stone traffic to the canal. Adjacent to the basin is Lime Kiln Cottage, one of the few remaining thatched buildings in Tiverton, now used as a tea room/garden. Also at the basin are modest visitor facilities with information concerning the canal, the country park and its wildlife, plus shop and public conveniences.

Horse-drawn trips by barge are a particular feature from April to October and a moored barge makes a fine and unusual tea room.

The Walk

The basic walk starts by Manley Bridge which has a variety of masons' marks on both parapets. Turn right along the tow path towards Tiverton. Unusually, this walk requires no route finding and no navigational directions are necessary. Look out for the badly eroded old "one mile" stone by the side of the towpath. The first bridge is Warniscombe, a flat, utilitarian farm accommodation bridge, followed by Tidcombe Bridge, an elegant and massive stone construction carrying a minor road, and a modern footbridge pro-viding access to a school. There is also the base of a long demolished bridge.

Views from the towpath embrace a wooded hill top to the south and high ground to the north, with a fair amount of Tiverton suburbia. The fine white building is Tidcombe Hall. The banks are largely tree lined and the vegetation includes abundant water lilies and irises.

The longer walk has the additional interest of Crownhill (or "Changepath") Bridge where the towpath crosses over, and an aque-duct constructed in 1847 over the former Tiverton to Tiverton Junction branch railway line. A cast iron trough is the basis of the aqueduct, carried on cast iron arches enclosed in brickwork. The choice of bricks for the renewal of the parapets is, to say the least, questionable. Another bridge is that at East Manley, with stop gate grooves adjacent. The "two mile" stone is passed.

The return in either case is by retracing footsteps.

2. Bickleigh

Length: 3 miles

Summary: A very easy, almost level, walk in the broad valley of the River Exe. The outward route is along the trackbed of a former railway line, with a return by a lane passing Bickleigh Castle.

Car Parking: Large free car park close to the entrance to the Devonshire's Centre at Bickleigh Mill. Grid reference 938074.

Map: Ordnance Survey Landranger no. 192, Exeter and Sidmouth, 1:50,000.

Tea Shop

The decor of the Bickleigh Mill Tea Shop is of good quality and stylish. The smart wooden tables and matching chairs are strong and practical whilst the wall lights and shades are of an unusual design.

Mid-day meals are imaginative and include the "Farmer's Lunch" with salad, ham, and apricots or the "Countryman's Lunch" of smoked Devon lamb with mint jelly. There is a choice of home-made cakes including rich fruit or chocolate shortbread; cream teas are also available. The usual selection of beverages is offered. When lemon, instead of milk for the tea, was requested, it was quickly and willingly substituted.

Open 10am – 4.45pm (last orders) every day from Easter to mid-Nov. and on Saturdays and Sundays only during the other months. Tel – 01884 855419

Description

Bickleigh Mill is a considerable tourist attraction, with craft centre, farm, gift shop, catering and a trout fishery. It is open during January to March on Saturdays and Sundays from 2pm to 5pm and from

Bickleigh Mill

April to December daily from 10am to 6pm Bickleigh village, with traditional cottages and a 15th century church, is close to the mill.

On the far side of the river is Bickleigh Castle, with a Norman thatched chapel and a three storey gatehouse which includes a great hall. It is open to the public from 2pm to 5pm on Wednesdays, Sundays and Bank Holidays in Spring, then daily until early October, excluding Saturdays.

The long disused railway line was a branch of the Great Western which connected Tiverton to the West Country main line a few miles north of Exeter.

The Walk

Set off along the straight, level footpath which is obviously the trackbed of the former railway line, through a gate at the end of the car park. The way goes in a straight line down the middle of the Exe valley, with the river to the right. Although without variation, this

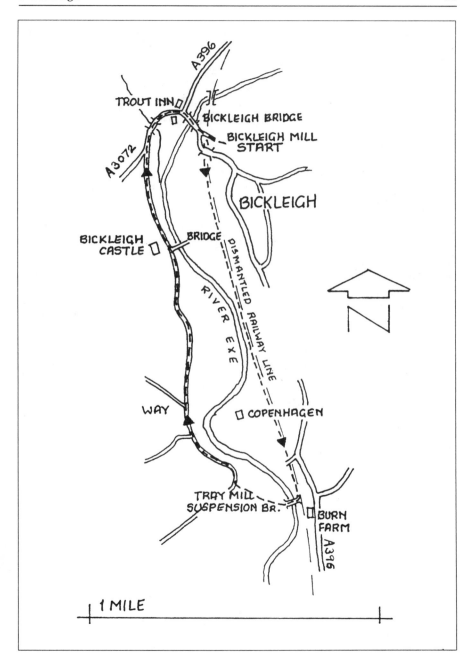

is a pleasant walk, with Bickleigh village on its pretty, wooded hillside to the left and Bickleigh Castle visible to the right.

A few gates need to be opened and for a short distance the quick flowing river is close to hand. Pass a former platelayer's hut and cross a surfaced lane with a gate on each side. About 150 metres before reaching Burn Farm turn right, by a tin shack, and cross the river on a lovely suspension bridge just two planks wide and swaying gently as one crosses. There is a reassuring handrail.

Head across the field to a gate on the left of the obvious buildings of Tray Mill to join a surfaced lane. Turn right and continue past Higher Tray Mill. Go straight ahead at a junction and stay with this extremely quiet lane, fringed by bramble and with plentiful butter-flies in the summer. Bickleigh Castle is soon reached. Just after passing the entrance to the castle a substantial bridge on the right permits a good look at the wide, swift river. A former footpath across the opposite meadow is no longer available.

Continue along the road, for some distance close to the river, well wooded with plenty of ash, until a more major road is joined. Turn right, cross a bridge and bear right towards the "Devonshire's Cen-tre". On the right is the Fisherman's Cottage Hotel; on the left the Trout Inn. Join the main road and turn right to cross the Exe on the old, rather narrow, five arched bridge. The last lap has more traffic but is mercifully short. After the bridge bear left immediately into the private road giving access to the Devonshire's Centre and the car park.

3. Ottery St Mary

Length: 2½ miles

Summary: A gentle stroll through the meadows of the Otter valley, never far from Ottery St Mary. The walk lends itself well to combination with visits to the church and other attractions such as Cadhay. Some moderately rough ground underfoot.

Car Parking: Pay and display long stay car park on Caanan Way, Ottery St Mary. Grid reference 097955.

Map: Ordnance Survey Landranger no. 192, Exeter and Sidmouth, 1:50,000.

Tea Shop

The Olde Coffee Pot in Ottery is not only a cafe but sells "collectibles" – one can browse amongst the bric-a-brac whilst waiting for tea. A particular speciality here is the Ottery scone – this product is heart-shaped and contains apricots. There is a legend attached to the recipe that tells the tale of two lovers – just ask and a copy of the story will be produced. Also on the menu are filled jacket potatoes, ploughman's lunch, clotted cream teas, etc.

Open 10.30am – 4.30pm all the year but closed on Sundays. Tel: 01404 815027

Description

A busy but generally rather workaday town in the broad, flat valley of the River Otter, Ottery St Mary's main claims to distinction are the superb church and the links with Samuel Taylor Coleridge.

Much of the church, including the twin towers, is a reduced scale copy of Exeter Cathedral, just a few miles down the road. The 14th century reconstruction by Bishop Grandison included a college for 40 monks, later dissolved. From the same period is the ancient clock in the south transept, one of the oldest in England but still in working condition. The interior of the church is packed with other features including fine vaulted roofs, one of the oldest lecterns in the country, many elaborate tombs and brass portraits.

Outside the church is a wall plaque to Coleridge. His father was the vicar here and Coleridge was brought up at Chanter's House, nearby. Warden's House and Vicar's House are two other good old dwellings in this area.

An altogether different attraction in Ottery St Mary is a circular tumbling weir, probably unique, at the large old mill at the bottom end of the main street.

Most of Cadhay House was built by the De Cadheney family about 1550, retaining the great hall of an earlier house. There are later Georgian additions. In 1996 the house and gardens were open to the public from 2pm to 6pm on the Sunday and Monday of the Spring Bank Holiday, Tuesday, Wednesday and Thursday during July and August and the Sunday and Monday of the late Bank Holiday.

Near Ottery St Mary

The Walk

From Caanan Way car park ("The Land of Caanan") turn left along the minor road, a pleasant lane with little traffic. The watercourse by the car park is a long leat feeding the Otter Mills (see "tumbling weir" above). Pass Dunkirk Cottages, bear left at Cadhay Bridge Farm and continue to Cadhay Bridge.

Cross the River Otter, then Talewater Bridge over the tiny River Tale. Next comes a former railway line, the long defunct Budleigh

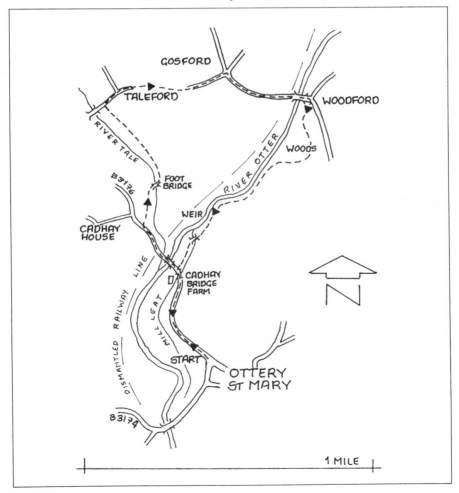

Salterton and Exmouth branch. By the trackbed is the former crossing keeper's house. Remarkably, the crossing gates are still in place.

Cadhay House comes into view to the left. Before reaching the drive to the house turn right at a signposted stile with yellow arrow to take a path which is just apparent across a flat meadow. Cross the River Tale by a substantial footbridge. The route remains obvious, over a stile and heading for Taleford Farm. A gate by a cottage and a willow tree gives access to a short lane and the public highway

Turn right to pass through Taleford hamlet. The quiet lane narrows before reaching a more important road by Gosford House. Turn right. Cross the former railway line again, with another crossing keeper's cottage, then the River Otter on a brick built bridge.

Fifty metres after the bridge turn right at a public footpath sign and follow the direction indicated by a yellow arrow towards the river bank. In 100 metres fork left away from the river and climb the bank into dense woodland. Leave the wood at a stile and bear right along the edge of a meadow. At the next arrowed stile re-enter riverside woodland. Within these woods the path is well defined but is somewhat rough underfoot and could well be slippery in wet weather.

A more open section follows another stile. Ascend the bank on the left, aided by wooden steps. At a fork either route will do, the way to the right being less overgrown. Descend to a large pool and weir, where the main leat feeding the mills half a mile or so downstream commences. Cross the leat and continue along a well used path to rejoin the outward route by Cadhay Bridge Farm.

Turn left to return to Ottery St Mary.

4. Colyton

Length: 6 miles

Summary: An almost level circuit, touring the water meadows of three rivers, the Axe, the Coly and the Umborne..In some places the footpath is not evident on the ground but the directions should avoid any route finding problems. There are no problems underfoot, but one short section is a little overgrown. The length of road from Whitford Bridge to Seaton Junction is quiet.

Car Parking: Pay and display car park in the middle of Colyton, by the public conveniences. Grid reference 248940. Alternatively, there is informal car parking beside Whitford Bridge. Grid reference 262955.

Map: Ordnance Survey Landranger no. 192, Exeter and Sidmouth, 1:50,000.

Tea Shop

The Olde Corner Shoppe is a good venue for tea – there has been a tea shop here for many years. The menu is small but adequate. There is a choice of both sandwiches and cakes; the scones served with clotted cream and fresh strawberries can certainly be recommended. For something different, try cinnamon toast. Daily newspapers are available to read whilst enjoying refreshments.

Please note there are only four tables in this tea and craft shop. If walking in a group you will be welcome but it would be advisable to telephone in advance.

Open 9.30am – 5pm. Out of season closed all Sundays and on Wednesday afternoons. In the winter months closed each day between 1 and 2pm. Tel: 01297 553129

Description

Colyton is a charming old town focused on its Market Place and

Tram at Colyton

adjacent church. For such a small town there is a good selection of "real" shops, not primarily visitor orientated as is the case in so many holiday areas. The church is very fine indeed, with its eight sided lantern rising above the older tower. The interior is light and airy, largely 15th century but with a 13th century chancel. The rich variety of monuments includes work of the 15th 16th and 17th centuries.

Whitford is a quiet backwater. Close by, at Whitford Bridge, is a popular riverside car parking/picnic area.

The now defunct Seaton Junction station stands rather forlorn on the London and South Western Railway (later Southern Railway) main line from London Waterloo to the South West, for many years competing with the Great Western Railway for the trade to and from Exeter, Plymouth and Cornwall. Important trains such as the Atlantic Coast Express passed by daily. The line is still operational but with only single track and in a much reduced capacity.

From the junction a branch line ran to Seaton, serving Colyton and Colyford on the way. Happily, following the inevitable closure of the line, the trackbed from Seaton to Colyford was taken over for operation as the Seaton Tramway. The line was later extended to Colyton. Working as a visitor attraction from Good Friday to the end of October, this 2' 9" gauge tramway uses a fleet of scaled down near replicas of trams from famous tramways such as Glasgow and the Isle of Man. The attractive ride along the side of the estuary of the River Axe is particularly recommended for observing the rich variety of waterfowl.

The Walk

From the car park turn right down Dolphin Street and continue along the obvious through road. Just short of Umborne Bridge turn right at a footpath sign to pass several small industrial units and reach a kissing gate with yellow arrow. Carry on along a worn path to a footbridge and cross the River Coly, burbling happily between its tree lined banks.

Note the East Devon District Council diversion plans, displayed at the next kissing gate, and continue by the side of the river along the broad bottomed valley with gentle low hills on each side. Just before the next kissing gate turn left at an "East Devon Way" finger post and go along the edge of the field to another kissing gate. Go through and turn right then, in 30 metres, turn left at a footpath sign which is largely obscured by nettles.

Cross the dyke on a wooden bridge, go over a stile and cross a big meadow diagonally to reach the embankment now carrying the Seaton Tramway. Don't go under the obvious bridge but continue alongside for a short distance to steps. Use these to cross the tramway. Avoid speeding trams and go right to descend. Head for a stile and then cross an arable field, possibly having to negotiate a crop of maize about 2½ metres in height! Going round the right hand edge of the field may well be preferable.

Emerge at a stile and turn left along the public highway, Tye Lane, lined with honeysuckle and bramble. Lower Cownhayne Farm is

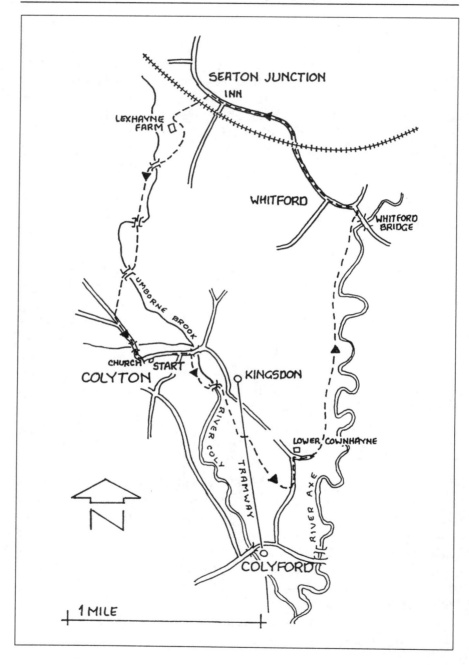

SEATON JUNCTION
INN

LEXHAYNE
FARM

WHITFORD

WHITFORD
BRIDGE

UMBORNE BROOK

CHURCH   START
COLYTON   KINGSDON

RIVER COLY

TRAMWAY

LOWER COWNHAYNE

RIVER AXE

N

COLYFORD

1 MILE

reached in less than a quarter of a mile. Turn right at a public footpath sign, soon reaching a stile with yellow arrow,

A succession of stile and gates, most waymarked with yellow arrows and the East Devon Way sign, now leads towards Whitford. For much of the way there is little evidence of a track on the ground and one or two of the stiles are not the easiest to find. Much of the way is close to the tranquil waters of the River Axe which meanders very considerably, obviously in no hurry to meet the sea. When the farming complex of Nunford Dairy comes into view keep well to the right and cross Nunford Lane to continue much the same line towards Whitford.

The public road is reached beside Whitford Bridge, where the superb picnic area is on the far side of the road. Turn left to walk through the village, going straight on at road junctions. Pump Farm at the first junction is a fine thatched structure with unusual curved frontage. The road is happily quiet, even in August, as it rises to pass under the railway. Carry on to Seaton Junction, a rather sad looking collection of no longer used railway buildings. Opposite the station is the Shute Arms Inn. Pass the industrial buildings at the station and turn left to cross the line by the second footbridge, with public footpath sign.

Descend to head across a meadow towards Lexhayne Farm. The path heads a little to the right of the farmhouse. By the farm turn left along the concrete driveway and, 100 metres beyond the farm, turn right as indicated by a yellow arrow on a post, through a gap in a tall hedge. Bend right to cross an informal caravan site, aiming for a bridge in the bottom left corner. Despite the possibility of a bull in the next field, cross the bridge and head boldly for a newish bridge ahead, crossing the River Usborne.

After this bridge turn left to follow a just evident path by the bank of the river as it hustles and bustles to its confluence with the River Coly and on the sea. After a stile there is an area of poor land rich in thistles and, at least in August, butterflies. The path is never far from the river, more audible than visible. Cross another footbridge, with gates, and go diagonally across the corner of a field to a stile.

Colyton is well seen rising up its hillside ahead, with the lanterned tower of the church prominent. Go diagonally right across the next field to another gated footbridge. Cross the river again, turning left. The path along the edge of this arable field is rather overgrown and could cause problems for those who walk in shorts! Go over more stiles then, at the last field, slant right to what appears to be the top corner, above the buildings of Road Green Farm.

Go through a gate to join a surfaced road and turn left to head for the church, crossing the River Coly for the last time. Fork left to the town centre, the tea shop and the car park.

5. Branscombe

Length:	2 miles
Summary:	An invigorating mini walk full of interest. Steep, hard ascent of West Cliff at start. Good path throughout.
Car Parking:	Sizeable car park (payment) at the end of the road at Branscombe Mouth. Grid reference 208880.
Map:	Ordnance Survey Landranger no. 192, Exeter and Sidmouth. 1:50,000

Tea Shop

Almost all properties owned by the National Trust close from November to April each year; an exception to this is the Old Bakery at Branscombe. As recently as 1987 brothers Stuart and Gerald Collier ran the bakery using old fashioned methods. When the National Trust acquired the property it was soon realised that, in order to comply with current law, the premises would need up-dating and this would inevitably result in loss of character. So a compromise was reached; the baking room has stayed as it was when the Colliers lived and worked here whilst the other rooms are now used as a cafe. The work has been sympathetically carried out. Therefore, apart from the need to refresh the body, one derives great interest from the environment and the artefacts on display.

In the cafe some unusual drinks are available including locally made apple juice, dandelion and burdoch, elderflower cordial, also good coffee, tea, etc. Sandwiches, ploughman's lunch with a choice of Stilton, Cheddar, or ham, and other savouries are served. Also a variety of cakes, for example, carrot and walnut or apricot and cinnamon. Scones are served with jam and clotted cream.

Open 10.45am – 4.15pm every day throughout the year. Tel: 01297 680333

The Masons' Arms, Branscombe

Description

Spread along the lower slopes of three separate combes which come together at Branscombe Mouth, the delightful Branscombe village is inevitably rather scattered. Despite being accessed only by narrow lanes, it is a place which attracts many visitors, the old Mason's Arms Inn being a hugely popular focal point.

Much of the village is separated from the nearby sea by the sheltering height of West Cliff, along the top of which this walk is routed.. The parish church, situated at the western end of the village, has a Norman tower and a Tudor gallery with external access stairs. Box pews and a most unusual three-decker pulpit are also among the features of this attractive church.

The Old Forge and the Old Bakery are both owned by the National Trust. The latter is now a teashop, selected for inclusion in this book, but was still in use as a bakery using entirely traditional ovens and equipment until the owners retired in comparatively recent times. The Forge has a recorded history going back over several centuries.

Branscombe Mouth has a shingle beach, well used by fishermen. There were formerly lime kilns and a coalyard supplied by boat.

The Walk

From the car park head for the sea and turn right at the tarmac road, passing the Sea Shanty restaurant (formerly the coal yard). The formidable West Cliff, with the Lookout Hotel, now confronts. Turn right at a kissing gate with National Trust sign to start the ascent. Kink left at a yellow arrow, rising more steeply, with the path not too well defined on the ground. Aim for a kissing gate in the top boundary of the field.

The views back along the coast and inland to Branscombe should make all this hard work worthwhile!

Beyond the kissing gate there are steep steps and a now clear path continues close to the top of the steep cliff – not a place for young children to run unsupervised. The excellent path continues through

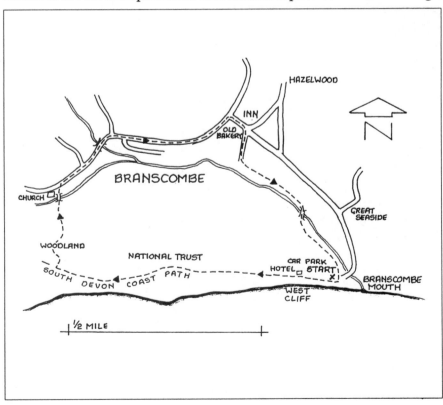

the upper edge of mature woodland as it bends inland, close to the top of a fine ridge with an occasional glimpse of Branscombe through the trees. Hereabouts there are holes in the ground resulting from the historic extraction of flints.

Eventually the path levels out by a stile. Keep straight on at the first junction of paths by another stile as the National Trust land is left behind and the path descends gently. As a metal mast comes into view turn right, downhill, then left immediately at two posts with yellow arrows to descend more steeply, reaching steps which continue the descent through mixed woodland which includes larch.

Go over a stile and along the edge of a field to reach Branscombe church. Cross the churchyard to the main gate and turn right down the road, passing the post office on the way to the Old Bakery, set back on the right. Almost opposite is the Old Forge, still used by a registered farrier, with a showroom for wrought ironwork.

From the teashop turn right along the surfaced road, then right again in a few metres into a cul de sac signposted "link to public footpath Branscombe Mouth ¾ mile". At a crossways of footpaths go straight on towards Branscombe Mouth. At a National Trust sign "Manor Mill. Footpath to sea" go through a little gate.

The track is well used over grass along the bottom of the combe alongside a swift running stream, with probably a little mud in wet weather. A tributary stream is crossed near a gate before the path kinks right then left to cross the main stream. Continue along the bottom edge of woodland, pass a small sewage works, and return to the car park.

6. Sidmouth and Salcombe Regis

Length: 3½ miles

Summary: A well varied circuit combining coastal path, woodland, riverside path and a visit to a holiday town. First rate paths and a small amount of road. Long ascents and descents, quite steep in places.

Car Parking: Any car park in Sidmouth town centre. Typical grid reference 875127.

Map: Ordnance Survey Landranger no. 192, Exeter and Sidmouth, 1:50,000.

Tea Shop

The views of Sidmouth Bay from the terrace of Salcombe Regis House are lovely and the atmosphere is very peaceful. Service on the terrace, or in the tea room, is attentive and helpful; walkers are very welcome indeed. The choice of food includes home-baked flan with salad, fresh crab sandwiches – it is always attractive and appropriate to eat crab whilst sitting with a view of the sea - cakes, scones, and crumpets. Choice of tea including, Ceylon, Kenyan, Earl Grey, etc. or try the summer tea; this is made from large leaf Darjeeling flavoured with fruit, flowers, and spices; it is preferably drank without milk in order to appreciate the flavours.

Open 12 noon – 6pm on Wed. Thurs. Fri. and Sat. and from 3pm – 6pm on Sundays. However, it would be advisable to check to avoid any disappointment. The Davey family have only recently moved to the property and are considering varying the hours.

Accommodation available, and walkers are welcomed. Tel: 01395 515993

Description

Beautifully situated at the mouth of the valley of the River Sid and sheltered by high headlands on each side, Sidmouth has always

Tea on the terrace: Salcombe Regis

been regarded as a rather "genteel" seaside resort, the lack of a sandy beach acting as a deterrent to those looking for more robust family holidays. There was substantial development during the early part of the 19th century when, among other distinguished visitors, the infant Queen Victoria stayed for a long period at what is now the Royal Glen Hotel in 1819/20.

The town hasn't changed much in the meantime and remains quite attractive overall with bustling shopping streets in season. There are many architecturally elegant buildings largely in Georgian and Regency period styles and a local museum in Church Street. The inland suburban sprawl of the present century can only be described as unfortunate.

Salcome Regis is a very small village situated high in its own steep sided valley leading to the sea. The rather grand "Regis" suffix results from the ownership of local land by Kings in Saxon times, one of the kings being Athelstan. The church has a Norman arch outside the chancel wall and Norman pillars on the north side of the wide nave. The tower is 15th century. Buried here is the 19th century astronomer Sir Norman Lockyer; his observatory, open to visitors, is found on the top of the nearby hill, close to the line of this walk.

The Walk

From any car park in Sidmouth walk to the main shopping street and head inland as far as the cinema. Turn right into Salcombe Road and cross the River Sid on a road bridge. Immediately on the left is the old toll house. Turn left to follow the asphalt path through the public park (Sid Meadow) alongside the River Sid, which has an impressive weir.

Continue for about half a mile, passing a footbridge and stepped weirs. On reaching the bottom end of a lane (Sid Lane), turn right to rise to a more important road. Turn left and then, in less than 200 metres, turn right into Milltown Lane. This lane is surfaced initially, rising steadily past a few houses. At the end of the surfaced section a "public bridleway" sign points the way.

The ancient track, a route used by farmers to and from the mills by the river, rises remorselessly between high hedges, meeting overhead to create a tunnel-like effect. At a waymarked fork, the yellow arrow points the way, left, up rudimentary steps for a steep short cut. Rejoin the original bridleway, turn left, and continue to rise along a lovely track under mature beech trees straddling the raised bank on the left of the track.

On reaching a more open area the track at last levels and the domes of the Lockyer observatory can be seen on the right. A public road is reached at a gate. Go across diagonally right to a kissing gate and carry on along a marked track through pine forest, with masses of bramble along the way. The path starts to descend. Turn left at a finger post "link path to Soldier's Hill". This path continues the descent, more minor but always clear on the ground.

At the top of a flight of steps, with finger post, turn right to descend the steps. Bear right at a junction, with glimpses of the lovely Salcome Regis combe, to reach an unmade lane. Turn left and on reaching a surfaced road bear left, uphill, to Salcome Regis church and the tea room at the cross roads above.

Return past the church along the lane signposted to the beach. In 200 metres or so fork right into the rough lane signposted "public footpath to Sidmouth". Pass the link path to Soldier's Hill used on the outward route and continue along the lane, with occasional views of the combe and the sea.

At a fork with a signpost "Sidmouth 1½ miles" go right, uphill. The correct route here is up a few steps to a little gate. The path rises easily through the woods, primarily pine. Turn left at a "T" junction. At the next junction turn left again. There is a signpost a little to the right of this junction "public footpath Salcombe Hill Cliff via Frog Stone". Go through a kissing gate and then fork right slightly uphill to a farm gate and unmistakable path along the edge of a field.

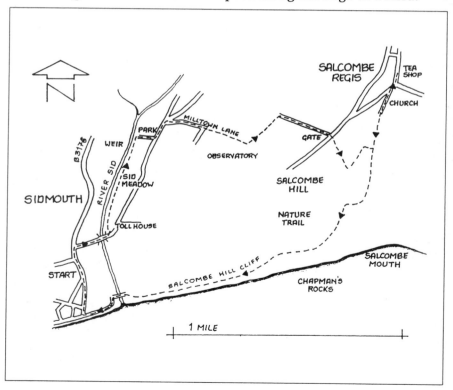

After another gate the path follows the cliff top with wide open sea views. Gorse and bramble are dominant as the official South West Coast Path rises up steps to join our route by a big stone (the "Frog Stone"?). Note the acorn waymark. Continue via a farm gate to a stone on the right dedicating South Combe Farm including the cliff summit as a permanent open space. Nearby is an orientation table listing the remarkable range of cliffs and other features, including part of the French coast, within view on a clear day.

After the orientation table take the middle of the three paths and begin the long descent to Sidmouth, largely through woodland of fairly recent planting. This descent is steep but is helped by many rudimentary steps. At the next junction go left "coast path, Sidmouth". After the woodland the views over the town and along the coast are marvellous.

At the lower end of this descent the traditional path has been affected by a cliff fall and in 1996 was closed by the Planning Authority on a temporary legal order, expiring at the end of October. Unless some necessary remedial work has been carried out, the Order is likely to be extended. If so, the inland diversionary route is well signposted – follow the arrows and acorns via Lasky's Lane and Cliff Road, turning left back towards the sea as soon as possible to reach Alma Bridge over the river.

Named after a Crimean War battle of 1854, the history of the bridge is given on a nearby blue plaque. Cross the bridge to the shingle beach, with a few fishing boats and their bits and pieces of machinery still evident. Walk along the promenade to return to your car park.

7. Otterton

Length: 6¼ miles.

Summary: This walk combines a length of the South West Coastal
                  Path with a popular track beside the River Otter and an
                  attractive village. There are no problems underfoot and
                  the total rise and fall is quite modest.

Car Parking: Informal parking area with space for about 12 vehicles.
                  Accessed from the Budleigh Salterton to Newton
                  Poppleford road (B3178) at the edge of the Budleigh
                  Salterton built up area via a minor lane across flat
                  estuarial land and a bridge over the River Otter,
                  leading to South Farm. Grid reference 075830.

Map: Ordnance Survey Landranger no. 192, Exeter and
                  Sidmouth. 1:50,000

Tea Shop

The Duckery Restaurant is part of Otterton Mill Craft Centre and
Museum. Another building in the complex houses the bakery. All
the bread, cakes and scones served in the cafe are prepared here in
the bakehouse from flour ground in the mill, so the food is com-
pletely home-made. The scones, newly baked and brought across
the mill yard to the tea room are especially memorable. Good coffee
and a variety of teas including Lapsang, Assam, or for a change, try
one of the herbal teas.

The decor is simple with vinyl cloths on the tables and a flag floor.
At the time of our visit the walls were adorned with very artistic
photographs which were available to purchase.

Open 10.30am – 5.30pm each day from Easter to 31st October;
11.00am – 4.00pm each day from 1st November to Easter. Tel: 01395
568521

Description

The attractive estuary of the River Otter has a nature reserve managed by the Devon Wildlife Trust along part of its east side, opposite the built up area of Budleigh Salterton. In this reserve are bat boxes among the trees and an old wartime pill box retained for bat nesting purposes. The estuary is also a noted feeding area for a variety of wild fowl.

Whilst the cliffs are not particularly high or spectacular, the length of coast from Danger Point to Smallstones is a bracing walk with long views towards Sidmouth, without the strenuous ups and downs which mar so many lengths of coast path for those who prefer gentle walking. In view are the sandstone cliffs of High Peak and Salcombe Hill, with the chalk of Beer Head more distant.

Otterton is not a showpiece village but it is quietly attractive with the possibly medieval water powered Otterton Mill as its principal feature The mill includes a craft centre, gallery and the recommended tea shop. Also in Otterton are the scanty remains of a priory founded by King John and the large parish church of St Michael, with 15th century tower as its oldest feature. A stream flows beside the main street for some distance and there are surviving 16th and 17th century dwellings of traditional thatched construction.

The Walk

From the car park turn right to leave the surfaced road by a pair of cottages, along a well marked path towards the sea. South Farm is soon visible to the left, nestling beautifully in a fold in the ground. Cross a wooden bridge and continue by the side of the estuary, above a narrow belt of weather battered conifers, part of the nature reserve.

Turn sharp left at the headland, close to the old pill box, and rise gently along the coast path. Behind, the view includes Budleigh Salterton and Straight Point. The low sea cliffs have gorse clad slopes, with areas of recent erosion and there are wide open spaces of cultivated land to the left. Follow this path for about 1⅓ miles, passing Black Head, Brandy Head, Crab Ledge and the back of Chiselbury Bay, none of them particularly pronounced. There is also

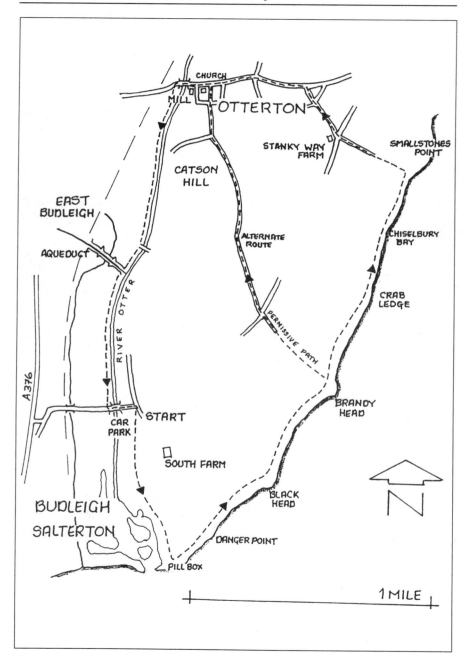

Budleigh Salterton from near Otterton

a former World War II lookout building by the side of the path. There is a little up and down but the walking is generally easy.

Turn left from the coast path almost opposite Smallstones Point, then left again at a stile, traversing a possibly muddy area before reaching a surfaced road leading to a junction at Stanky Way Farm. Turn right to follow the road downhill, passing two junctions, straight to the top of Otterton village street, close to a service station. Turn left downhill. The mill complex is on the left at the bottom.

After refreshment cross the river on the road bridge and turn left to follow a signposted path towards Budleigh Salterton along the far side of the river. This excellent path stays close to the river for about 1 mile leading back to the bridge which carries the lane giving access to the car park. Part way along this route there is an interesting aqueduct still carrying water across the valley. Cross the river and return to the car park.

(The walk may be shortened by turning left off the coast path at a permissive path signpost which leads via a cul de sac road straight to Otterton village)

8. East Budleigh

Length: 4½ miles

Summary: An attractive walk to and from a fine village, generally on green lanes and good footpaths. A high heathland common and woodland are included. The route passes by Sir Walter Raleigh's birthplace at Hayes Barton.

Car Parking: Free public car park with public conveniences in Hayes Lane, East Budleigh, below the parish church. Grid reference 066849.

Map: Ordnance Survey Landranger no. 192, Exeter and Sidmouth, 1:50,000

Tea Shop

A venue off the main tourist track is The Old Granary Tea Room at East Budleigh. The decor here is quite whimsical, for the shop is full of teddy bears of all descriptions, as well as other charming animals, and all are for sale to "good owners"! Even the chairs at unoccupied tables have teddies sitting on them! The furniture is white and the crockery and table linen is of pleasing design.

Hot meals such as ham and eggs, grills, fish, etc are served all day. For tea there are cakes, cream teas, or even a " knickerbocker glory". On Sundays a roast lunch is served between 12 noon and 2pm.

Open 12 noon – 5pm all the year but closed on Mondays. Tel: 01395 445919

Description

East Budleigh village is sufficiently off the tourist beaten track to be unspoilt, with many cob and thatch buildings remaining. Flower bedecked throughout the summer, it is no surprise to learn that the village is a powerful contender for "Best Kept Village" awards.

The mainly 15th century church of All Saints has the Raleigh family arms (Sir Walter's father was churchwarden) on one pew;

there is an unusually good array of secular carving on many others. Raleigh's birthplace, Hayes Barton, is a beautifully kept cob and thatch Tudor farmhouse of impressive size. Unfortunately, it is not at present open to the public.

The Walk

Walk back to the High Street and turn right. Cross the stream, which then runs prettily beside the road. In about 400 metres, opposite a small school, turn right at Wynnards Farm. Pass the farm buildings and commence to rise along an unsurfaced lane. This green lane has every appearance of being an ancient trackway as it climbs steadily between high hedge banks.

Go straight on at a staggered junction. The track narrows and is slightly overgrown as it levels out, now with more open views. Immediately to the right is the edge of Hayes Wood, predominantly young conifers on this fringe. A similar lane joins from the left and the ground becomes distinctly sandy. Carry on, bearing right, uphill, to reach the edge of East Budleigh Common, part of an extensive area of heathland. Gorse and heather are now the dominant vegetation, with plenty of bramble.

At the top of the rise turn right, slightly downhill, at a broad stony junction, soon passing a high brick wall, apparently part of a former shooting range. Continue along a very broad track with Hayes Wood still close on the right, to reach a minor surfaced road by a log vehicular barrier.

Turn right. Hayes Barton farmhouse, attractive and immaculate, is on the left in a short distance, unfortunately no longer open to the public.

(To continue along the entirely peaceful public highway provides a direct return to East Budleigh and a shorter walk overall)

For the full circuit, less then 100 metres after the farm buildings turn right at a farm gate to follow a wide track giving access to Hayeswood Cottage, just visible at the edge of the wood. Bear right immediately after the cottage and enter the attractively mixed woodland on a wide rising track. At a fork bear right to follow yellow

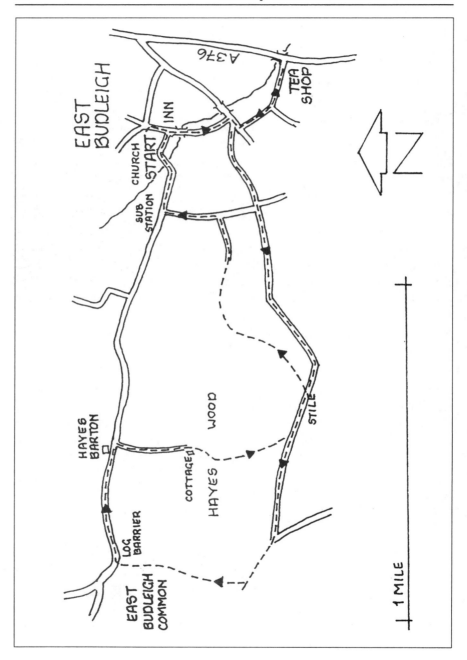

Raleigh's birthplace, Hayes Barton

arrows, still rising. Go straight across at a junction and descend to rejoin the outward route by a large log.

Turn left along the path for more than a quarter of a mile, to a stile with "public footpath" post. Turn left to take a marked footpath over open pasture, in total contrast to the earlier part of the walk, with splendid long views over East Budleigh to high ground above Sidmouth. The path meanders round the top of the hill above the village to a stile before bending right to descend to a gate/stile, and then along the edge of an arable field to another gate/stile and a green lane.

Turn left to descend to the surfaced highway (Hayes Lane) opposite an ugly electricity substation. Turn right to return to East Budleigh, passing Hill Farm and the 15th century Vicar's Mead which has a good thatched wall. For centuries this house was the vicarage.

For the tea shop turn right at High Street and follow the curving street almost to the junction with the main Newton Popplewell to Budleigh Salterton road. The tea shop adjoins an inn.

9. Shaldon

Length: 5 miles

Summary: Quite a demanding circuit with a fair amount of ascent. A mixture of coastal path with lanes and some roadside walking. Only the 400 metres or so on the Teignmouth to Torbay road is subject to a significant amount of traffic.

Car Parking: Large pay and display car park beyond the far end of Marine Drive, Shaldon. Grid reference 939719. Use the upper (far) end of the car park if possible.

Map: Ordnance Survey Landranger nos. 202, Torbay and South Dartmoor (70%) **and** 192, Exeter and Sidmouth (30%).

Tea Shops

Here we give a choice of two cafes and both are fully recommended:

The Old Bakery at Stokeinteignhead is part of the way round the walk; this delightful tea room was one of those surprise finds. The building is very old – mainly 18th century but the lower walls have been dated 14th. There is a shady vine-clad terrace – super when visiting on really hot days. Miss Taylor, the proprietor, serves home made soups, including cock-a-leakie, with crusty bread, cheese onion and potato pie, plum cobbler, filled nectarine with red currant sauce – all very tempting. There are also the award winning cream teas or the savoury tea which includes cheese scones. The home baked confectionery includes sticky date cake, carrot cake and apricot and oatmeal squares.

Open 12 noon – 6pm Easter to the end of Sept. Closed on Mondays. Tel – 01626 873442

The Chequered Lantern is equally pleasing and can be found on the delightful main street in Shaldon. It is open for morning coffee, lunches (between 12 noon and 1.45pm) and afternoon tea. Service

The Olde Bakery

is very pleasant even when arriving, as we did, five minutes before closing time! The food is well prepared – try the home-made apple pie with clotted cream – and the prices are very reasonable. Paintings displayed on the walls are by Devon artists and are available to purchase.

Open 10.30 – 4.45pm all the year but closed all day on Thursdays and on Sunday mornings. Tel – 01626 872384

Description

Facing Teignmouth across the estuary of the River Teign and with a steep wooded slope behind, Shaldon is a large linear village with a surprisingly unspoilt charm. Perhaps the small print used for the name on the ordnance survey maps has something to do with the comparative lack of visitors! One main street with a few shops, an inn and tea room, terraces of attractive cottages with plentiful floral displays, and the ever changing views across the estuary all contribute to making Shaldon a most appealing little place. At the sea end of the main thoroughfare is the Ness, a great wooded headland. From this end of the village a foot ferry plies to and from Teignmouth

Stokeinteignhead (sometimes this rather unmanageable name is separated into its three components) is a totally unspoilt village sitting low in a combe a little way inland. Among the lovely thatched buildings are inn, tea shop and post office. The parish church has a fine old chancel screen and particularly good sandstone pillars with carved capitals among its many interesting features.

The Walk

Walk towards the seaward end of the large car park. Beyond the car park turn right to go uphill along a stony track. Just to the left is a viewpoint area, with seat. Turn left to ascend steps (waymarked) and emerge from the woodland along the bottom edge of a golf (pitch and putt?) course

Go over a stile and continue along a superb grassy path soon climbing steeply again before reaching the main road at a gate/stile. There are just a few metres more of coast path before a trudge of more than 300 metres along the roadside, regrettably unavoidable.

Turn right into a surfaced lane, Commons Lane, again rising substantially to reach "The Beacon" (168 metres – 552 feet). Turn left at the top into an unsurfaced lane lined with bramble and honeysuckle. Go left at a fork and descend gently towards Stokeinteignhead. Reach a surfaced road by a farm then join the public road, turning right into the charming village. The Old Bakery Tea Rooms are on the corner opposite the Church House Inn. It is hard to believe that this village is only 3 miles from the hustle and bustle of Newton Abbott.

Turn right here, then right again at the next junction into Forches Hill. Take the second lane on the left, well up the hill, by the Stokeinteignhead boundary sign. This sandy looking lane continues, with some up and much more down, for more than one mile towards the estuary of the River Teign, with some good viewpoints in the latter part across to Bishopsteignton and the estuary.

Turn right at the Newton Abbott to Shaldon road and walk by

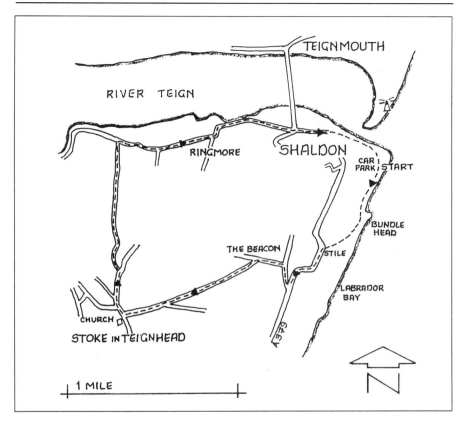

Ringmore back to Shaldon. Fortunately this is quite a minor road with occasional distractions such as watching the trains on the former Great Western Railway West of England main line on the shore opposite and a first view of Shaldon bridge.

At the main road junction go straight across into the principal street of Shaldon. Continue past shops, inn, tea room, public conveniences and ferry and follow Marine Parade to the Ness House Hotel. Leave the road and go to the left of the hotel to take the South West Coast Path (acorn and yellow arrow), initially up steps.

The views of Teignmouth and the boating activity are fine, particularly from an official viewing point. Bear right here, downhill through woods, to reach the upper end of the car park.

10. Bovey Tracey

Length: 6 miles

Summary: A circuit through woodland and open country combining lanes with good footpaths and the trackbed of the former Newton Abbot to Moretonhampstead branch railway line. Some mud, but not excessive: long ascent at start.

Car Parking: Main car park by Tourist Information Centre at lower end of Bovey Tracey. Grid reference 813782.

Map: Ordnance Survey Landranger no. 191, Okehampton and North Dartmoor area, 1:50,000.

Tea Shop

Riverside Mill, complete with working wheel, is now used as a craft centre. The old mill yard makes an attractive and very sheltered spot to enjoy refreshment after completing one of the more strenuous walks in this collection. If indoors is preferable, the Granary Tea Shop is charming. Paintings (available to purchase) are displayed on the walls, fresh flowers adorn each table, whilst the bright, clean, attractive food counter tempts the appetite with salads, quiches, and baskets piled high with rolls; hot savouries include a Devon pasty. Try the unusual Dartmoor rocky cake – it is recommended! Tea and coffee is good quality – for something different there is Lusscombe cider.

Open all the year except Bank Holidays in winter 7 days a week from 10am – 5pm. Tel – 01626 832223

Description

Bovey Tracey is an attractive "genuine" town with a long shopping street rising from the former mill by the River Bovey. Right at the top of the town, the church is basically 15th century, with a 14th century tower. Inside, there is much fine carving, most notable being the screen, one of the best in Devon, with 31 apostles painted on the lower panels.

The railway line connecting Moretonhampstead with the Great Western Railway main line at Newton Abbot was constructed in 1866 to the broad gauge of 7 feet favoured by the great Brunel and his associates. In common with the rest of the Great Western Railway it was converted to standard gauge towards the end of the 19th century. Inevitably under used in more recent times, the line was closed in 1959.

The Granary Tea Rooms

The Walk

Walk up the hill along the lengthy main street of Bovey Tracey. Just before reaching the church turn left into Trough Lane and climb steadily (and quite steeply!) up the surfaced lane. As the road bends right, go straight ahead into an unsurfaced lane between high hedges. The occasional gateway allows good views back over Bovey Tracey. As the gradient eases, cross a potentially muddy section before joining another very minor road.

Stay with the road, uphill, along the edge of woodland, passing the entrance to Beech Leigh Farm. Go straight on at cross-roads (Furzeleigh Cross). Pass a horse riding centre and Lower Bowden Farm then turn left at a stile signposted "public footpath County road near Slade Cross" The route across a field is not marked on the ground, but follow the line indicated by the signpost to a gate/stile in the far right corner.

Proceed along an old lane, cross a tiny brook and the drive to Shaptor Farm, to a waymarked stile opposite. Go over the stile and follow a fenced footpath behind the farm. After more stiles, Shaptor Woods are reached (The Woodland Trust – visitors welcome). A good track traverses the attractively mixed woodland, with the rock of Shaptor above. A plaque dedicated to G. Hurrell 1901-1981 is passed and the track descends to the left by an old stone gatepost (orange waymark)

At the bottom turn right at a signpost, still heading for the County road near Slade Cross. Just after a Hawkmoor Water Supply post go straight across a broad cross track, then cross a small stream by a waterfall. The path narrows beside bramble; keep right at what appears to be a junction. There are more "path" signs, a stile, and a farm gate. Turn right, then left at once to another sign post and gently descend through open countryside towards a farm complex, the path being immediately to the right of a farm trackway. Continue around the upper edge of the farm to join a minor road. Turn left to reach the Bovey Tracey to Moretonhampstead road at Slade Cross.

Cross over to the minor road opposite and rise for a short distance. Stay with the road, bending left for a long descent past Hatherleigh

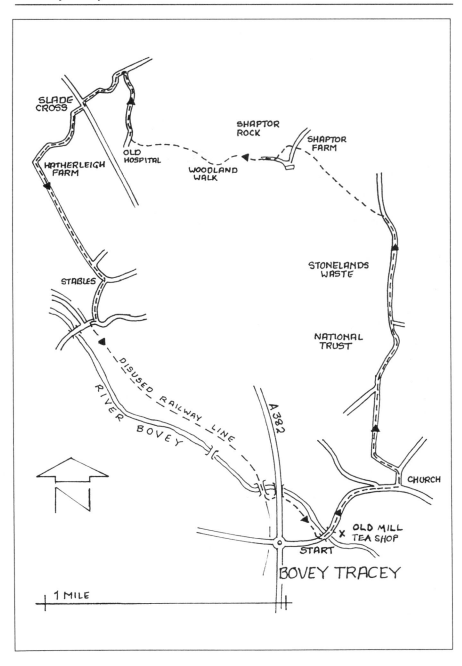

SLADE
CROSS

SHAPTOR
ROCK

SHAPTOR
FARM

OLD
HOSPITAL

HATHERLEIGH
FARM

WOODLAND
WALK

STONELANDS
WASTE

STABLES

NATIONAL
TRUST

DISUSED RAILWAY LINE

RIVER BOVEY

A 382

CHURCH

N

OLD MILL
TEA SHOP

START

BOVEY TRACEY

1 MILE

Farm. In about one mile, by a horse riding establishment, turn right at a junction signposted "Moretonhampstead; Bovey Tracey" and follow the road along the side of a stream, soon reaching a gate close to a redundant railway bridge, with a broad track rising to the former line.

Continue along the trackbed to the outskirts of Bovey Tracey. Cross the River Bovey and go through a kissing gate to reach the by-pass road. Cross over, go through another kissing gate, and follow a grassy track close to the river across a substantial recreation area, taking care not to disturb the adders allegedly lurking along the river bank! The main street in Bovey Tracey is reached close to the car park. The Granary tea room is across the road in the old mill complex.

11. Lustleigh

Length:	5½ miles
Summary:	Although of modest length, this is quite a demanding walk with considerable ups and downs. There are some rough sections underfoot and in summer bracken encroaches on part of the route towards Hunter's Tor.
	Much of the walk is through woodland, but the views from the approach to Hunter's Tor and from the Tor itself are excellent.
Car Parking:	Roadside spaces in Lustleigh village. Grid reference 784813
Map:	Ordnance Survey Outdoor Leisure no. 28, Dartmoor, 1:25,000 **or** Landranger no. 191, Okehampton and North Dartmoor area, 1:50,000.

Tea Shop

Primrose Cottage in Lustleigh is a picture-postcard English tea room and one not to be missed; people come back time after time. Morning coffee, lunches, cream teas, cheese teas (scones served with Stilton or Cheddar and fresh fruit, plus tea or coffee), toasted tea-cakes, delicious home-made cakes and biscuits, are all served throughout the day. At lunchtime one may have a more substantial dish such as salmon and broccoli bake, or Devon ham served with new potatoes and salad. When the weather is suitable take the opportunity to choose a table in the garden overlooking the river.

Open 10.30am – 5.30pm Easter to the end of October and weekends in winter (the hours could change; if in doubt just telephone first). Tel – 01647 277365

Description

Lustleigh is a lovely village situated in one of Dartmoor's best fringe

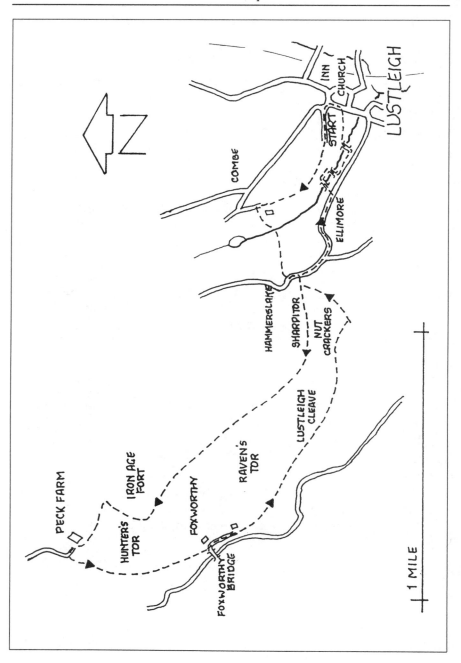

areas, where the sides of the deep cut river valleys, richly woodland clad, climb steeply towards impressive rocky tors.

At the heart of the village the largely 15th century church has earlier features and also a carved 16th century screen. Nestling close to the church are the Cleave Inn, Primrose Cottage tea shop and the post office/stores. The Moretonhampstead branch railway line, opened in 1866, passed through Lustleigh, bringing considerable numbers of visitors before its unfortunate closure after World War II.

Lustleigh Cleave (cliff) is the name of the rocky slope rising from the River Bovey to Hunter's Tor and the broad ridge which runs south east from the tor. Although the opposite side of the same valley has its own "cleave" names – Neadon, Horsham and Water – the whole valley is now generally called "Lustleigh Cleave" The Lustleigh side of the valley has become progressively more wooded over the years and has a rich and varied plant and bird life. From Victorian times, particularly after the arrival of the railway, the Cleave has been immensely popular as a "romantic" landscape.

The Walk

From the upper side of the church take the road rising to a junction, with the Old School House in the angle, and turn left along a "road unsuitable for lorries". In 30 metres go left at a footpath signposted to several places, including "Cleave". Follow the stony lane. By the last house go through a kissing gate into a little meadow with a huge granite boulder.

At a junction of paths by a gate go straight on. Enter woodland by another kissing gate, the track being overgrown in part. At a gate by a house emerge on to a surfaced roadway. Turn left at a battered sign "Hammerslake for the Cleave". Pass the front of the house to a gate with a yellow circle and cross a swift running stream among lush vegetation.

The path now rises for some distance through rough woodland, partly on large mossy stones with care needed. At the top a stile gives access to a minor road. Turn left for 25 metres then turn right at a bridle path "Lustleigh Cleave" sign. A sunken lane rises to a stile/gate and signpost. Bear a little right towards "Hunter's Tor". Continue to rise through woodland on a well defined path. The overhanging rock on the left is the "Donkey's Cave".

Partial emergence from the woodland close to Sharpitor is followed by a good viewpoint on the left. Hereabouts was the "Nutcracker", a poised logan stone which could be rocked to crack hazel nuts until it was displaced by vandals in 1951 and broke up when attempts to reinstate it were made. Much of the valley of the River Bovey and the high ground on the far side are in view.

The next section of the path suffers from encroachment by bracken, aided and abetted by some bramble and gorse. Plough on along the ridge. Another granite outcrop provides a fine perch for the reasonably sure footed. Trees hereabouts – primarily oak but with some rowan – seem to be somewhat small and stunted. Continue to rise towards Hunter's Tor, with views now widespread, including Manaton village, Moretonhampstead and Hound Tor.

As Hunter's Tor is approached gorse becomes the dominant vegetation, with some heather. The path divides a few times but this is of little significance. Just before the tor is reached, the banks and ditches of an Iron Age fort are apparent. Views from the tor include the famous Hay Tor, Rippon Tor, Hound Tor and Easdon Tor.

Carry on through the gate, slanting right downhill on a good path. Join a wider track and turn left to reach Peck Farm. Go through a gate and bear left. In 100 metres or so turn left again at a gate.

An inviting track leads through the bracken and the bramble, terracing nicely above the cultivated part of the Bovey valley. An ancient stone wall/bank on the left accompanies this path for a considerable distance. Go through a gate to reach the well renovated structure of Foxworthy Farm. Go right, then left at a signpost "public bridlepath Hammerslake" etc. *Just below, to the right, the River Bovey is crossed by Foxworthy Bridge.*

The path passes the entrance to Foxworthy Mill. Keep right then, in a few metres, go left at a signpost to a gate and continue through woodland, close to the river. Go straight on at the next signpost and commence a long ascent through the woods, with plenty of silver birch. Look out for lizards and butterflies in this area.

At a signposted "T" junction turn left, passing large boulders along the way. Rejoin the outward route at a signposted junction and turn right to descend to the surfaced road. Turn right to follow this entirely quiet road. Turn left at the first junction to descend steeply past Ellimore Farm, which has a range of old stone buildings. In a quarter of a mile turn left to leave the road at a signposted broad track into woodland, cross a stream, then turn right immediately before a kissing gate to cross the stream again among a jumble of great mossy boulders – care here!

At a meeting place of several tracks keep left to a gate and a bridge over the stream. Head straight for Lustleigh church across an amenity area littered with large boulders to emerge by the post office and return to your car.

The tea shop at Lustleigh

---

12. Castle Drogo

Length: 4¼ miles

Summary: A most attractive walk including Castle Drogo and a
                wonderful part of the valley of the River Teign. A long
                ascent but fine paths throughout. The upper part of
                "Hunter's Path", with its viewpoints, must rank among
                the very best in the whole of Devon.

Car Parking: By Fingle Bridge, accessed from Drewsteignton by a
                minor cul de sac road. There are public conveniences.
                Grid reference 743899.

Map Ordnance Survey Outdoor Leisure no. 28, Dartmoor 1:25,000 **or**
        Landranger no. 191, Okehampton and North Dartmoor
        area, 1:50,000.

Tea Shop

Castle Drogo was built by a wealthy Indian tea baron, Julius Drewe,
so it is appropriate to include the refreshment facility here in a book
of tea shop walks.

The modern reception area houses the ticket sales counter, shop
and restaurant. The latter is large, with a slate floor, attractive
furniture, and ceiling to floor windows opening to an outdoor area
with tables and benches shaded with huge umbrellas. The facilities
are of a high standard; the service helpful and pleasant (even at 4pm
on a busy summer Sunday!). There is a good choice of food – ham,
cheese, turkey rolls, jacket potatoes with fillings, meat pie with
salad, cakes, scones, etc.

Please note the restricted opening of this tea shop – linked to the
hours when Castle Drogo is open to the public.

Open 1st April – 31st October every day from 10.30am – 5.30pm.
Also limited refreshments available in November and December.
Tel: 01647 – 432629

Description

Built between 1910 and 1930 to the designs of Sir Edwin Lutyens for Julius Drewe, who had made a fortune with incredible rapidity in the Home and Colonial Stores grocery chain, the impressive granite pile of Castle Drogo is now in the ownership of the National Trust, although members of the family have continued in occupation.

With the castle is an estate of more than 600 acres extending over both sides of a particularly fine part of the valley of the River Teign, with thick woodland cladding much of the steep slopes. Fallow deer live here and are often seen during the daytime.

The house and gardens are open from 11am to 5.30pm, 1st April to the end of October. The reception complex has a car park, croquet lawn, recommended tea room, shop and plant sales.

Fingle Bridge is a well known beauty spot and picnic area a little way downstream, where a tributary has cut a gorge which allows a minor road to reach the bridge. By the river is the Angler's Rest Inn, with a range of varied catering.

Hunters' Path and the Teign Valley

For those with a geological interest this part of the Teign Valley is noted for the coming together of granite – Hunt's Tor – and softer shales – Sharp Tor.

The Walk

From Fingle Bridge set off along the Fisherman's Path. From the roadside parking above the Angler's Rest this path is a right turn before crossing the bridge. The path is kept in first class condition by the Trust and is never far from the river as it meanders close to the valley bottom. Although the path divides and rejoins from time to time route finding is no problem.

The head weir which served Fingle Mill, now a ruin, downstream of the Angler's Rest, is passed as progress is made through the rich woodland. A rocky viewpoint is accessed by steep steps up and down, but can be bypassed by keeping left, close to the river.

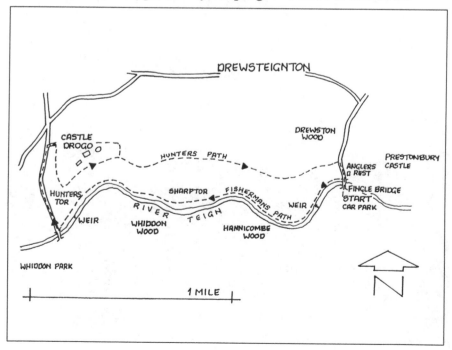

A building on the far side of the river is the turbine house, part of Lutyens's original design, providing electricity for the house. A little way further is a large weir, creating the head of water necessary to drive the turbines. After a further distance a footbridge is seen to the left and paths meet at a signpost. Turn right for "Hunter's Path. Road near Castle Drogo" and commence a long ascent, soon joining a surfaced road.

In about half a mile look out for a signpost on the right "Castle Drogo 0.5m". (One of the longest half miles in Devon!). Enter National Trust land through a gate. The end of the castle is just visible up to the left as a fine terraced footpath rises gently, with extensive views of the Teign valley. Heather and gorse are profuse on this hillside.

By the foot of a flight of steps turn left at a "Castle Drogo and Garden" signpost and rise steeply to the castle access road. Turn left and then fork right up to the car park for the tea shop.

After refreshment return along the car park access road to the right turn, signposted "Hunter's Path". Descend to the signposted junction, turn left to follow "Hunter's Path. Fingle Bridge" and go down steps to a "T" junction at a superb viewpoint from which much of the Teign Valley and part of the castle itself can be seen. Turn left towards Fingle Bridge.

The well used and maintained path clings to the steep valley side above the woodland. At two junctions keep right for Fingle Bridge, eventually reaching rather scrubby silver birch and oak woods as the path descends the valley side at an even gradient. One section is a little rough underfoot but there is no real difficulty.

Turn right at the Fingle Bridge access road to reach the inn, the bridge and the car parking.

13. Chagford

Length: 3¼ miles

Summary: A well varied little circuit, firstly over the height of
                 Nattadon Common and then down to the River Teign,
                 returning to Chagford along part of the Two Moors
                 Way, a delightful riverside footpath. Apart from some
                 encroachment by bracken, no difficulty underfoot.
                 A variation on the return section uses the Rushford
                 Steps across the River Teign.
                 The walk can be based on Chagford or on the
                 alternative car park mentioned below.

Car Parking: Free car park in Chagford. Grid reference 702875 **or**
                 Informal car park on the edge of Nattadon Common,
                 three quarters of a mile south east of Chagford along a
                 minor road leading to Middlecot. Grid reference
                 707867.

Map: Ordnance Survey Outdoor Leisure no. 28, Dartmoor,
                 1:25,000 **or** Landranger no. 191, Okehampton and
                 North Dartmoor area. 1:50,000.

Tea Shop

A range of hot dishes is offered at The Old Forge Tea Rooms; piping
hot jacket potatoes were particularly welcome on a raw March day.
The "Old Forge Grill" comprising bacon, mushrooms, egg, tomato
and chips also proved popular as did "Old Forge Coffee Break" – hot
potato cakes, cheese scone, and a mug of steaming coffee. "Old Forge
Tea Break" comprises toasted teacake, chocolate bar and pot of tea.
Other items are conventional cream teas, hot buttered crumpets,
Devonshire Farmhouse Ice Cream. There is a vast list of speciality
teas including Assam, Kenyan, and many others.

On Sundays a traditional roast lunch is served. It is advisable to
pre-book. Open every day all the year (closed on Wednesdays out
of the main tourist season) from 10am – 5pm Tel: 01647 433226

Chagford

Description

Although remains of the former mining activity in the surrounding countryside are by no means obvious, Chagford was one of the original four "stannary" (tinners' parliament) towns. With the square and its "pepperpot" market house as its lively centre, the compact town retains interesting old buildings. The parish church of St Michael has a lofty 15th century tower and painted screen of about the same time. Within a short distance are four inns, one of them of the 16th century, and a good range of shops including old-fashioned, all-purpose ironmongers.

The River Teign flows close by in a comparatively gentle section of its valley.

The Walk

Leave Chagford car park by the information board and pass across the front of the Jubilee Hall to reach the end of High Street by the church. Turn left into New Street, with attractive old terraced houses. Pass the old school. The street becomes Meldon Road.

In a little more than a quarter of a mile fork left into Nattadon Road. Fifty metres before the end of the houses on the left turn sharp left along a rising signposted track "public footpath Nattadon Common". Reach a signposted gate/stile, cross a stream and fork left, rising steeply and soon emerging on to the open hillside among tall bracken, awkward in summer. A part overgrown seat may be welcome part way up this long ascent. Height is gained rapidly and the views to the west are fine.

Despite the bracken the way is not in doubt; there is a fence on the left as the top is approached. Continue to the informal car parking area and join a surfaced road. Turn left over a cattle grid and, in 30 metres, turn right at a gate/stile signposted "footpath. road. Gt. Weeke". In a few metres go over another stile and turn left to keep close to the hedge, as advised, over rough grass. Kink right and then left to another stile at the bottom.

Stay close to the hedge on the left across the next meadow, with long views to the north. Join the remains of what looks like an

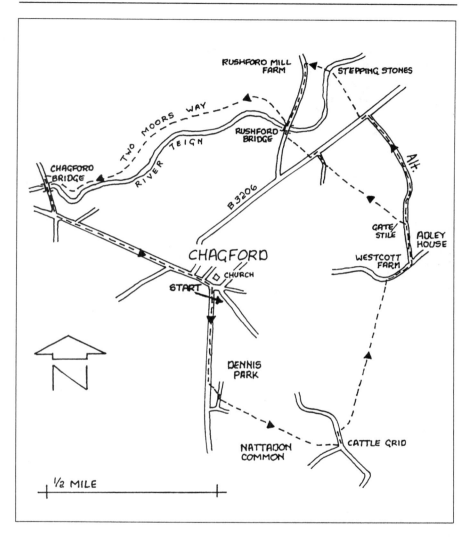

ancient lane and go straight on downhill among gorse and bracken, the path now better defined, to a gate and a sunken lane descending steeply to a minor road.

Turn right at the road, then left at Westcott Cross road junction into Adley Lane. In a quarter of a mile turn left at a wide opening.

For a slightly longer walk with the interest (and fun?) of crossing the river on Rushford stepping stones, continue along Adley Lane to the main road, turning left for 20 metres, then right to follow a "Rushford stepping stones" signpost. A narrow lane, somewhat over-grown, leads to a stile. Go over and cross the meadow to the left of the large oak tree to reach the steps across the River Teign. The water is not normally seriously deep but the steps are not the easiest and some moss does not help. The odds against at least one boot full of water are probably about evens.

With wet or dry feet pass Rushford Mill Farm, turn left at the road and walk towards Rushford Bridge. Near the bridge, take any path on the right to rejoin the basic route on the Two Moors Way.

The wide opening leads to a gate/stile in a few metres. Go diago-nally across the field to a stile in the far bottom corner. Keep much the same line across the next field to reach a small built up area at a stile (Neighbourhood Watch!). Go over another stile and follow a broad residential driveway to the main road.

Turn left. In 60 metres turn right at a stile with "footpath Rushford Bridge" signpost, soon reaching another stile and the road over the two-arched stone Rushford Bridge. Cross the bridge and turn left over a signposted stile. Cross a riverside meadow to another finger post, turning left beyond the hedge. At a mini footbridge, stile and signpost head for "Chagford".

The route now keeps fairly close to the river for more than half a mile, over stiles and little footbridges and through gates. It is an entirely delightful section of the designated "Two Moors Way", linking Exmoor and Dartmoor. Towards the end of our section of the path there is a curious line of trees, beech and oak, growing out of the tops of stone plinths.

The path reaches a road near the ancient Chagford Bridge. Turn left to cross, then left again at a road junction to ascend quite steeply through a leafy highly desirable residential area back to Chagford. In the town centre, the tea shop is found by turning left for a short distance from the square. The car park is reached by continuing along High Street. The fine old buildings opposite the churchyard include a narrow alley, with the former cinema.

14. Buckland Beacon

Length:	4½ miles
Summary:	A good combination of the rocky tor of Buckland Beacon and the tiny village of Buckland in the Moor, with its interesting church, craft centre and thatched cottages. There is a fair amount of ascent, mostly on good paths or minor roads. The descent from the Beacon is rather rough in parts.
Car Parking:	Small car park on Buckland Common at the cross-roads known as Cold East Cross. Grid reference 741743.
Map:	Ordnance Survey Outdoor Leisure no. 28, Dartmoor 1:25,000 **or** Landranger no. 191, Okehampton and North Dartmoor area 1:50,000.

Tea Shop

The Round House Craft Centre is part of a farm complex owned by the Perryman family since 1946. There are numerous craftsmen producing goods for inspection and possible purchase and the tea shop which is run by members of the Perryman family.

As well as teas with Devon clotted cream there are delicious ice cream dishes such as triple tutti-frutti, strawberry swans, or lemon zing. Those feeling hungry can eat very heartily here with a tempting menu including ham, egg, and chips – tempting! – especially to those who have enjoyed a good walk. The atmosphere is most friendly with members of the Perrymans happy to chat to visitors about the farm and the family.

Open: 9.30 – 6pm – seven days each week all the year except the week before Christmas but re-opens on Boxing Day. Tel: 01364 653234

Description

Surprisingly in view of its modest height of 1282 feet, Buckland

Beacon is renowned as a viewpoint. Below is the wooded valley of the River Dart with, on a clear day, the waters of the English Channel beyond. In the other direction the high moorland hills roll away to the horizon. In 1588 a fire was lit on the tor to signal the sighting of the Spanish Armada. Another great fire celebrated the Silver Jubilee of 6th May, 1935. According to a nearby inscription the assembled crowd shouted "God Save the King"

More curious, however, are the two large stone tablets at the foot of the rocks, engraved in 1928 with the Biblical commandments, by order of the then Lord of the Manor of Buckland.

In the tiny village the 15th century church has a lovely painted screen and a clock with letters which form "MY DEAR MOTHER" instead of numerals on its face. Nearby, a group of thatched cottages is so typical of South Devon that the scene must have adorned the lids of a million chocolate and biscuit boxes. The Round House craft centre and tea shop have been imaginatively converted from farm buildings.

Cottage, Buckland in the Moor

The Walk

From the car park turn right along the road signposted to "Ponsworthy". In 200 metres or so turn left. There are three tracks heading across Buckland Common. Take the one to the left. Note the old boundary stones in this area. On approaching an informal car parking area by a cattle grid, veer a little to the right to join a major path by a wall.

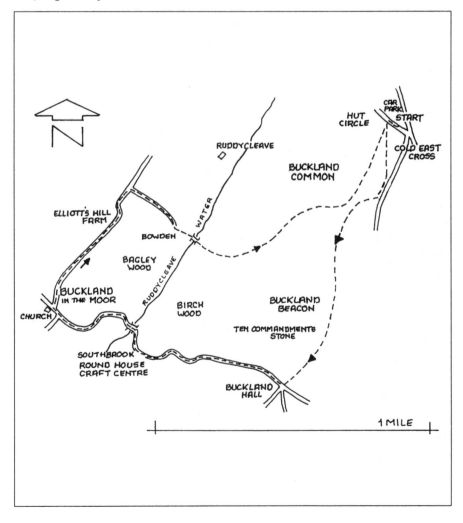

Continue towards Buckland Beacon, a minor tor which soon becomes evident ahead. The broad, very easy, track keeps close to the wall for most of the way to the summit. The Beacon provides a superb viewpoint and has the added interest of the stones with the Commandments and the plaque recording the use of the tor as a prominent place for the lighting of a signal bonfire. The adjacent vegetation is rich in bilberry.

The next section of the walk is less easy. A definite path stays fairly close to the wall on the left, but weaves around among the ever encroaching bracken, descending quite steeply. However, the route is never really in doubt, passing under a short line of ash trees part way down. Reach a gate and continue through a short section of woodland to the road opposite the entrance to Ausewell and Woodland Cottages.

Turn right. In rather less than half a mile the Roundhouse Craft Centre, including the Horse Wheel Cafe, is reached.

After an appropriate visit continue along the road through Buckland. On the right are beautiful thatched cottages before the road rises to the church. Turn right into Elliots Road, a long cul de sac serving a handful of farms. This surfaced lane climbs steadily to pass Elliots Hill Farm. Turn right shortly after this farm, soon reaching Bowden Farm.

Bend left here, cross a little stream on a bridge, and rise again along a slightly sunken lane by the edge of a wood. At the top a gate opens to Buckland Common, a favoured place for Dartmoor ponies. Many tracks cross the Common. The required line is to bend a little left, but to angle away from the wall on the left. A well used track takes this line. Ignore various cross tracks and continue almost to the wall which was followed on the outward route.

Bear left 20 metres or so before the wall to take a well marked track passing two of the old boundary stones and heading in a straight line to the Ponsworthy road. Turn right at the road to return to the car park.

15. Dartmeet

Length: 6 miles

Summary: A fine circular tramp around the favourite gathering place where the West Dart and East Dart rivers come together in beautiful surroundings. Both river valleys are visited and there are three crossings on good easy stepping stones. Paths are good, the views superb, and the short road sections are very quiet indeed. There is a reasonable amount of ascent but no very steep gradients.

Car Parking: Large free car park at Dartmeet, with public conveniences, refreshments and gifts. Grid reference 673733.

Map: Ordnance Survey Outdoor Leisure no. 28, Dartmoor, 1:25,000 **or** Landranger no. 191, Okehampton and North Dartmoor area, 1:50,000.

Tea Shop

Brimpts is one of the original Dartmoor settlements. It has been farmed since 1307. It is still a working beef farm. In the farmhouse one can have good quality food at sensible prices. The atmosphere is pleasantly informal in the dining room and all the food is cooked in the farm kitchen. Produce is obtained locally and therefore the menu will vary from season to season. Home-made soup with roll and butter is always available. Hot dishes offered include beef pies, jacket potatoes, and hot-pots. Afternoon tea includes home-made scones and Devonshire clotted cream together with hedgerow and blackcurrant jams.

Everything here from a quick coffee to a three course Sunday roast lunch (advisable to telephone for menu and availability).

Open: March to October every day from 11 – 6pm. Hours may vary depending on school holidays etc. If in any doubt please telephone first. Tel: 01364 631250

Stepping stones over the West Dart River

Description

Sitting below the 368 metre (1208 feet) height of Yar Tor, Dartmeet has always been one of those favoured places with fine river scenery embedded well into the heart of the generally desolate moor. Stepping stones and clapper bridges feature in this lovely walk and there are numerous opportunities for riverside picnics and family recreation.

Close to the car park, Badger's Holt, now a catering complex, was originally a fishing lodge belonging to an ancient manor. The area is rich in remains such as hut circles whilst clapper bridges such as that close to the present road bridge are of great and generally unknown antiquity.

The Walk

Set off back towards the public road. Turn right and cross Dartmeet Bridge. The ancient clapper bridge is just downstream of the present bridge. Turn left at a former petrol filling station to a signpost. Follow "Holne Road or Comberstone Tor", forking left at once to stepping stones across the West Dart. Note the warning about heavy rainfall!

Climb the valley side on a good path, with occasional blue circle waymarks to confirm the route. The path rises steadily over farm land towards Comberstone Tor. At a junction by Comberstone go straight ahead, still rising. The views from this high ground are extensive, including Dartmeet, behind.

More open moorland is reached as the way levels, with piles of stones evident. Comberstone Tor is to the left, ahead. Pass a deep depression on the right to a signposted junction. Turn right to "Week Ford Stepping Stones for Huccaby ¾ mile" For a short distance here the path is not too distinct as it goes downhill, but after a gate in the wall it is much more obvious

On approaching the West Dart there is swampy area and two broken walls are crossed as the track bends left to a three-way signpost. Go left for "Huccaby via Stepping Stones". Go through a gate and cross a bridge over a stream to reach the stepping stones –

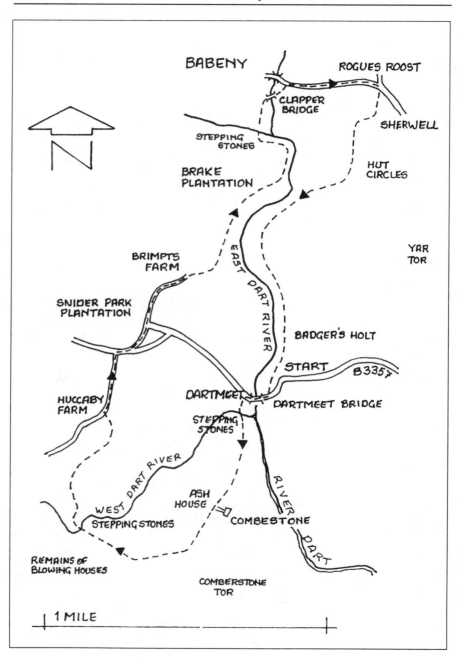

good, solid, large stones, únlikely to be a problem unless the river is in spate.

At a three-way signpost take the "Bridlepath Huccaby", with a blue circle. The excellent path rises steadily, with views across to Hexworthy. At a junction with two signposts bear left downhill to a gate. Turn left to the public road. Turn right and walk to the main road. Turn right for 200 metres or so then fork left at the entrance to Forestry Commission land, with a Brimpts Farm board setting out the varied catering.

Fork right at once in the woodland and follow the broad driveway to its junction with the Brimpts Farm surfaced access road. Go left to continue to Brimpts Farm, now very much in the valley of the East Dart.

After the break carry on in the same direction (to avoid the farm, the path passes around the back and is well marked with signposts and blue circles). The wide track descends the open valley side towards the river. At a fork keep right, downhill. The ruin is that of the 18th century Dolly's Cottage. There is a legendary story about the occupation of this cottage, set out on a notice by a nearby gate.

A short section of the path now runs rather beautifully beside the river. At a signposted junction turn right to cross yet another good set of stepping stones. The shady track rises beside a tumbling stream. Cross the stream on an ancient clapper bridge. The path divides; either branch will do as they some come together again, rising to join an unfenced minor road.

Turn right to follow the road for about a third of a mile. Sixty metres after passing "Rogues Roost" (there must be a good local story here!), turn right at a stile signposted to "Dartmeet 1¼m.". Pass a waymarked electricity pole and aim for a gate. The next field has some rather swampy ground. Veer right to a waymarked little bridge and then a gate. Rise along the edge of a meadow, with Yar Tor above to the left. Go through a gate/stile to the open moor and a track through the heather.

The right of way shown on Ordnance Survey descends from this point diagonally and evenly to Dartmeet. On the ground, the trodden paths through the bracken, which soon takes over from the heather, are somewhat different. At a crossing of paths not much more than 100 metres after the gate the suggested route is to turn right, descending quite steeply. Although there are variations, there is never any doubt of a well used path through the bracken, heading for the broad riverside track visible below. Much of the descent is aimed just to the left of the Dolly's Cottage ruin situated on the far side of the water.

Turn left at the bottom and stroll past numerous alluring riverside picnic spots to Badger's Holt refreshment rooms. Go through this complex to return to the car park. Should Badger's Holt be closed and this way not be available, turn left uphill at the signpost, then right to pass behind Badger's Holt.

16. Holne and New Bridge

Length: 4 miles
Summary: A circular tramp over varied upland, partially on minor
                 public roads, not busy, to visit the pleasant, rather
                 off-the-beaten-track village of Holne, birthplace of
                 Charles Kingsley. The return route is by a lovely
                 footpath descending the side of the valley of the River
                 Dart, through National Trust woodland.
Car Parking: Public car park, information centre and public
                 conveniences at New Bridge, on the Ashburton to
                 Dartmeet road. Grid reference 711709.
Map: Ordnance Survey Outdoor Leisure no. 28, Dartmoor,
                 1:25,000 **or** Landranger no. 202, Torbay and South
                 Dartmoor.

Tea Shop

The Old Forge at Holne is pleasantly away from the main routes
across Dartmoor. Therefore it is quiet and peaceful to sit outside this
cafe on a sunny day, or if the weather is not too good, to be cosy
inside.

Anne Baker and her assistant willingly serve good food. There are
some unusual items on the menu including toast with Gentleman's
Relish or Marmite. "Breakfast" is served all day and includes hash
browns, two eggs, sausage, bacon and tomato. Local ham is served
with egg and chips or with salad. For afternoon tea there are
sandwiches, scones and cakes but do try the home-made meringues,
served with clotted cream from a nearby farm. Good choice of teas
including China and Assam.

The tea room is also open on Friday evenings to serve suppers.
No license but customers are welcome to bring their own wine and
there is no corkage charge.

Open: Easter to end of October – 7 days, 10.30 – 5.30 (plus Friday evenings). Also open some weekends out of the main season. Hours could vary depending on school half-term holidays etc. If any doubt just telephone. Tel: 01364 631351

Description

With a fine open situation high above the River Dart, Holne is a good Dartmoor village, retaining its shop, inn and tea room despite being away from main roads and, consequently, not overrun by visitors. Charles Kingsley was born here in 1819 at the Old Vicarage, a little way from the village. It has since been rebuilt.

The 15th century parish church has a screen with forty painted figures, said to be the work of monks from Buckfast Abbey a few miles away, a memorial window to Charles Kingsley and a particularly fine roof in the porch.

"New" Bridge looks very old indeed, a lovely bridge spanning the River Dart, so narrow that traffic along the road to Dartmeet and Two Bridges must crawl carefully across.

The Walk

Cross the bridge and walk up the road past "Pixieland". Turn right at once to go up a few steps to a stile. Keep left to stay close to the hedge as requested, up a long rising meadow, through a gap in an intermediate hedge. Go over a stile at the top and turn right at a minor road.

Walk past Chase Gate Farm. At the Stoney Post junction go straight on uphill towards Hembury Woods. At the next junction, Gallant le Bower, turn right towards Holne. In August the roadside banks were full of butterflies. In about half a mile, by a road junction turn left at the second farm gate to follow a broad track rising among gorse over Green Down. The views are the best so far, with Holne nestling attractively below the bulk of Holne Moor beyond.

Leave the Down at another gate and descend an unsurfaced lane to Ridgey Cross road junction. Turn left downhill towards Buckfastleigh. Go right at the next junction, descending more steeply. Immediately before the house on the right at the bottom turn right

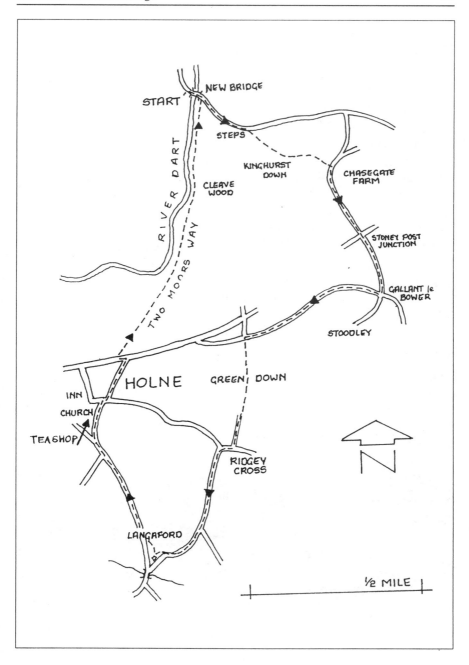

START

NEW BRIDGE

RIVER DART

STEPS

CLEAVE WOOD

KINGHURST DOWN

CHASEGATE FARM

TWO MOORS WAY

STONEY POST JUNCTION

GALLANT le BOWER

STOODLEY

GREEN DOWN

HOLNE

INN

CHURCH

TEASHOP

RIDGEY CROSS

LANGAFORD

N

½ MILE

on to a track with a tiny stream beside. In 30 metres turn left at a gate with public footpath sign and rise to a second gate. Continue to another gate and turn right, uphill, along a broad stony track, part of the Two Moors Way.

Join a surfaced road and go straight ahead. Bear right at the Holne boundary sign. The old Forge is on the left, close to the church.

Carry on along the road, passing the church and the Church House Inn. Go straight on at the cross roads, rising a little. Go left at the next road junction, signposted "Hexworthy". In 30 metres turn right over a stile with a public footpath sign and a "path to New Bridge" notice after the stile.

A good footpath now goes unerringly downhill from stile to stile, crossing meadows before the welcoming noise of a waterfall heralds the proximity of the river. Enter National Trust land, Holne Woods, at another stile. At a junction follow "New Bridge" along this delightful path. The road is reached at a gate. Turn left to cross the bridge and return to the car park.

Holne

17. Buckfastleigh and the Abbey

Length: 2½ miles

Summary: A short but interesting walk in an area packed with features such as Buckfast Abbey, the headquarters of the South Devon Railway, the Buckfast Butterflies and Dartmoor Otter Sanctuary and the old town centre of Buckfastleigh. Ascent of a long flight of steps at the beginning.

Car Parking: Pay and display car park in Station Road, Buckfastleigh. Grid reference 742662

Map: Ordnance Survey Outdoor Leisure no. 28, Dartmoor 1:25,000 **or** Landranger no. 202, Torbay and South Dartmoor 1:50,000

Tea Shop

The Grange Restaurant at Buckfast Abbey is a relatively new building. The pleasing architectural design is reminiscent of a monastic refectory. From the large windows, and the attractive terrace, there are impressive views of the River Dart and the monastery church.

A wide choice of food and drink is available at the self-service counter; the entire menu being available throughout the day. At mid-day on Sundays a roast lunch (the beef is from the Abbey farm) is a tempting option.

Open: All the year from 10am – 5pm but check the closing time if visiting in the winter months. Tel: 01364 42761

Description

Buckfast Abbey was founded in 1018, becoming a Cistercian community until the inevitable dissolution in 1539. The buildings then fell into ruin, only one tower and foundations remaining by the late 19th century. However, unlike hundreds of other decaying monastic sites, the ruins were purchased, in 1882, by a group of French

Buckfast Abbey

Benedictine monks. From 1907 the incredible story is of a band of never more than six monks steadily building the great edifice in local stone which we see today. Their dedicated toil was finished in 1938.

Whilst the exterior of the Abbey church is rather austere, much of the interior is lavishly furbished. The community is now thriving and is well organised to receive visitors in large numbers, daily apart from Good Friday and Christmas Day. Within the complex are the Grange restaurant, the Abbey gift shop, the Abbey bookshop, the monastic produce shop, a video presentation and an exhibition hall. The living quarters of the community are private, but all services in the Abbey church are open to the public. In front of the Abbey are two ancient crosses and a giant sequoia tree.

Buckfastleigh was a busy little woollen town on the River Mardle. However, for many years it has been by-passed by the Exeter to Plymouth road traffic and is now a comparatively quiet backwater with attractively narrow streets and alleys. The remains of the parish church stand on a hill high above the town, reached by an immense flight of steps. Most unusually for Devon it has a tall spire. The curious structure outside the door is the tomb of Richard Cabell, designed to confine the spirit of a reputedly thoroughly bad character. A ruined chapel stands close by.

Close to the line of the walk is the headquarters of the South Devon Railway, formerly the Dart Valley Railway, a long established preserved railway line, using steam locomotives as a visitor attraction from April to October and at other special times such as Christmas. Close to the station is the Buckfast Butterflies and Dartmoor Otter Sanctuary, open daily from early March to November, 10am to 5.30pm or dusk if earlier; March to October, 11am to 3pm.

The Walk

Turn right from the car park, cross a bridge and turn left to climb a flight of almost 200 steps. At the top is a gate and a welcome seat. Continue along a well used path to the remains of the parish church, destroyed by fire on 21st July, 1992. The ruins of a 13th century chapel are on the same site.

Turn left along the cul de sac road, pass Churchill Farm and carry on to a triangular road junction. Turn right and, in 20 metres, go through an old kissing gate on the right to follow a lightly used path by a hedge. After another kissing gate descend along a sunken path,

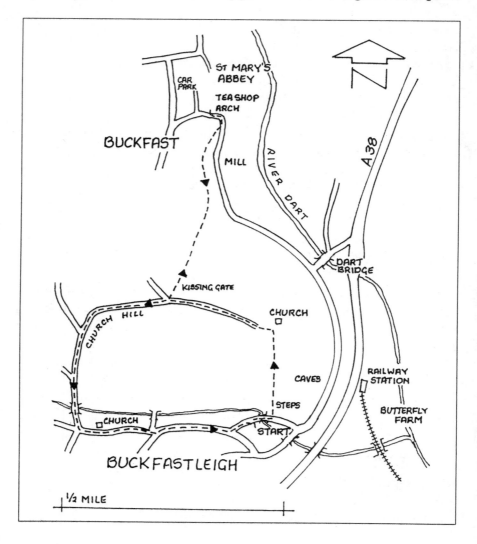

soon with a good view of Buckfast Abbey. After a third kissing gate descend to the main road

Turn left, pass Buckfast post office, pass the bollards and bear right under an arch into the Abbey grounds. The many facilities are spread around, the tea shop being directly opposite.

The best return route is to retrace your footsteps along the excellent path as far as the triangular junction. Turn right here and descend the narrow lane known as Church Hill, Continue past the Sun Inn, turn left and pass the Roman Catholic church to reach the main street. Turn left to return to the car park.

```
┌─────────────────────────────────────────────────────┐
│                                                       │
│              18. Dartington                           │
│                                                       │
└─────────────────────────────────────────────────────┘
```

Length: 2½ miles

Summary: A great little walk with no serious ascent, linking the
                lovely Dartington Hall complex with the major tourist
                attraction of the Dartington Cider Press Centre. Mainly
                on first class footpaths, the route avoids roads.

Car Parking: Several signposted car parks behind Dartington Hall, all
                accessed by the minor road leading from the main
                A384 road to the Hall. Typical grid reference 798628.

Map: Ordnance Survey Outdoor Leisure no. 20, South Devon
                1:25,000 **or** Landranger no. 191, Okehampton and
                North Dartmoor area, 1:50,000.

Tea Shop

The Cider Press Centre is busy and bustling with lots to see. Muffins
is an open air cafe in a sheltered position. It is pleasant to sit at one
of the rustic tables and to observe passers-by whilst enjoying refreshments. The menu is quite extensive and includes filled French
batons, Dartington ploughman's lunch with Sharpham Brie, Blue
Stilton, or ham. Cream teas, delicious cakes and of course muffins
are also available. Drinks include tea, coffee, fruit juice, and inevitably, cider.

Also in the Centre is Cranks. Here, one can choose from a range
of vegetarian dishes. For tea the choice of cakes is mouth- watering.
Try Devon apple cake, vanilla Swiss roll, or coffee and walnut cake.
Extra to the usual tea, coffee, fruit juice, etc. organic wine may be
purchased. All the food served here is baked on the premises.

Open: Muffins – Easter to October – every day 10am – 5pm; Cranks
– Easter to Christmas, every day 9.30am – 5pm but closed on
Sundays during the remainder of the year Tel: 01803 864171

Description

Situated less than two miles from Totnes, Dartington is a place of great historic interest and of many present day attractions. Firstly, there is the Elizabethan Dartington Hall, centre of a large medieval estate which was very run down when it was purchased by Leonard and Dorothy Elmhirst in 1925. Their intention was to re-create a whole range of traditional country activities, sparing no expense in the process. Since that date, developments have, indeed, been considerable. There is a well known boarding school and wide ranging adult education, whilst at the Hall itself, a roofless ruin in

Cider Press near Dartington Hall

1925, a major music school is held each summer. In the gardens the tilting yard has been beautifully restored and is used for a variety of events.

Agriculture and forestry have flourished and a whole range of commercial activity is centred on the Cider Press Centre, located close to Skinner's Bridge on the main road (A385). Included are a vegetarian restaurant (Cranks), Muffins tea shop, books, pottery, toys, farm foods, plants and above average gifts. Although cider is no longer produced, the farm foods shop does have a traditional local product.

Close to the line of this walk, at Staverton, is a station on the South Devon Railway, formerly the Dart Valley Railway, which was one of the first closed down branch lines to be restored and re-opened as a tourist attraction with steam locomotives.

The Walk

From any of the car parks walk along the road behind the Hall to reach Park Road. Turn into Park Road and head away from the Hall following the signpost to Warren Lane and Warren House. At a road junction fork left, still heading for Warren House.

On reaching a farm gate/stile with a "no cycling" notice continue along a lightly used footpath with an estate wall on the right. Long views include Staverton village and, if you are lucky, a glimpse of a passing steam train on the South Devon Railway. Go over another stile and along the edge of a wood. Follow wheel tracks diagonally left across a field to reach a rough concreted road which goes straight to and through the complex of Old Parsonage Farm.

At the public road turn right. In 200 metres turn left at a public footpath sign to follow a well made path leading directly to the Cider Press Centre, across a minor access road.

After using the various facilities, including the tea shop, continue along the footpath with the main road and stream close on the right, soon entering woodland. At a fork rise to pass behind a large building, then descend. A footpath joins from the right, having come over a bridge beside the main road.

Fork left, up two rudimentary steps, at once. A well established path rises through attractive woodland. Turn left at a junction with a red arrow on a post, rising to a stile and open country beyond. Aim to the right of the building ahead – the Dartington Horticultural Training Establishment. The well known school is now visible to the left.

Go over a stile and bear left to follow the hedge uphill, taking care to go over a stile on the right just after passing the horticultural training complex. There is another stile and a field before the Dartington Hall access road is joined, by a gate. Turn right for a few metres and then right again through a gate with red arrow, opening into the grounds of the Hall.

Follow the surfaced road to the Hall through the beautiful gardens. Shortly before the Hall a "private" sign is reached. To visit the church go up to the left. To admire the Hall and its immediate surroundings go right along a fine terrace, passing a celebrated line of twelve clipped yews. Turn left at the end of the terrace, pass the White Hart, and bear right at the courtyard to return to the car parking areas. If the main entrance is open a peep at the interior of the great hall is in order.

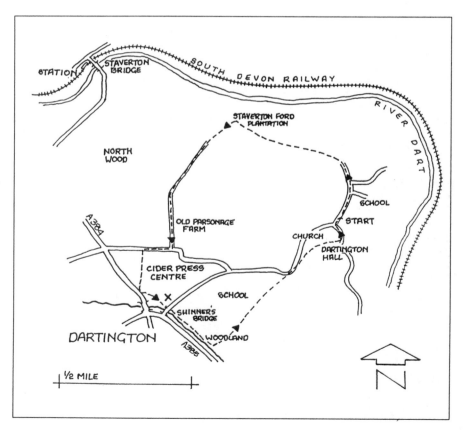

---

19. Cockington, Torquay

Length: 2¼ miles.

Summary: A remarkable little walk through woodland and farmland yet close to the heart of the Torbay conurbation. No serious ascent or difficulty underfoot.

Car Parking: Pay and display car park in Cockington village. Grid reference 894639.

Map: Ordnance Survey Landranger no. 202, Torbay and South Dartmoor, 1:50,000

Tea Shop

Wander through the garden gate and round to the back of Rose Cottage and one is surprised to find this large tea garden; the decor is stunning. Each season the owner, Paul Herbert, has a huge and very smart awning erected over the terrace thus providing a large and very sheltered dining area which can be used in all weathers. Visitors can play petanque or croquet in the garden and there is even a band-stand where live music, of the light classical variety, is performed from time to time.

Everything here is smart, clean, and inviting. The menu is extensive offering pizzas, omelettes, salads, selection of cakes, sandwiches, crumpets, and scones. Dishes of the day are chalked-up on a blackboard.

Open: 10 – 6pm everyday from Easter or 1st April to the end of October and possibly into November depending on the weather. Tel: 01803 606607

Description

The survival of the tiny old village of Cockington in its wooded valley so close to Torquay is entirely remarkable. Presumably it is also a triumph for modern Town and Country Planning which must

Rose Cottage tea shop

have prevented this haven from being submerged under the suburban development of the Torbay conurbation.

Within the village are a few old thatched cottages, an ancient forge, the former manor house Cockington Court and the adjacent church. Cockington Court is set in a large area of beautiful grounds, well maintained by the Borough Council, owners since the 1930s. Originally Elizabethan but much altered, the house is not particularly impressive. It is now used as a craft centre and for public refreshments. Sitting on a bank carpeted with snowdrops, daffodils and primroses in spring is the church, with 13th century tower. Inside, the 15th century screen has been much restored. Also within the village is the Drum Inn of 1934, designed by Sir Edwin Lutyens and the adjacent old Granary complex.

Inevitably, Cockington has become a very popular visitor centre; the present small Tourist Information Centre on the car park is likely to be replaced by a more permanent structure in the near future. In summer horse drawn carriages provide transport to and from the sea front.

The Walk

Turn left from the car park to pass the old granary, then turn right
to pass the forge. On the right is the former mill. Turn right at the
entrance to Cockington Court, pass the Higher Lodge with its in-
triguing first floor overhang, then fork left at a sign "Woodland Trail.
Lakes".

Pass through gardens with many fine shrubs and plentiful grey
squirrels. Go under a bridge which carries Totnes Road and fork
right at a sign "Gamekeeper's Cottage". At the cottage, now an
environmental education centre, leave the paved track to follow a
good path signposted "Woodland Walk. Warren Barn" rising gently
through Manscombe Wood to the barn, the subject of a major
restoration project.

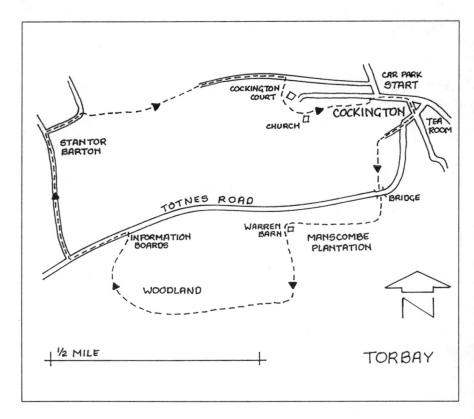

Just before the barn bend left up to a stile, signposted "Scadson Woods". Turn left along a path at the edge of a huge field. At the top go through a squeezer stile to a junction of routes. Bear right to another squeezer and a path signposted "Scadson Woods – horse riding route".

As the woods are entered the path forks. Either route will do as they eventually rejoin. That to the right keeps to the valley side and is marginally shorter. Keep straight on at a junction, following "Cockington via Totnes Road", soon reaching the road at an information board. Turn left along the road for about 400 metres and at the top of the rise turn right at a gate with public footpath sign. The "no dogs allowed" notice here is probably of dubious legality.

The path heads straight for a farm. At the farm keep left initially to a signpost. Turn right for "Cockington". The way ahead is now very obviously to a gate with signpost, then rising across a meadow. Further posts define the route through gateways and over stiles, with long views over much of the Torbay area.

The roofs of Cockington Court with the church beside are soon apparent below on the right. At a kissing gate with various posts go straight on, gently downhill, between a wall and a hedge. Turn right at a farm gate/stile, still a little way above the Court, to take a broad track descending into and through the cultivated gardens at the rear of the house. Continue past the house and the church to follow the surfaced drive back to the village, turning left to the car park.

```
┌─────────────────────────────────────────────────────────┐
│                                                           │
│              20. Churston (Brixham)                       │
│                                                           │
└─────────────────────────────────────────────────────────┘
```

Length: 4¼ miles (shorter version 3½ miles)

Summary: A surprisingly attractive walk mainly in the green belt
                 which separates Brixham from the rest of the Torbay
                 conurbation. Easy walking with very modest rise and
                 fall. Includes part of the South West Coastal Path.

Car Parking: Roadside spaces on the minor road by Churston church,
                 easily reached from the main A3022 Brixham to
                 Torquay road, via Churston Ferrers. Grid reference
                 904565.

Map: Ordnance Survey Outdoor Leisure no. 20, South Devon
                 1:25,000 **or** Landranger no. 202, Torbay and South
                 Dartmoor, 1:50,000

Tea Shop

Including "Ye Olde Churston Court Inn" in a book of tea shop walks
may be considered cheating. However, we wished to include this
particularly delightful walk and the inn does welcomes walkers. At
lunchtime there is a carvery table in the bar – pleasant to sit by the
fire when the weather is not too good – and sandwiches and other
light meals are also available. Cream teas are served during the
afternoon. Dinner and bar meals available in the evenings.

Large garden to the front of the inn, with tables and benches for
sunny days. Open: usual licensed hours. Tel: 01803 294565

Description

Space does not permit a description of the huge range of visitor
attractions spread over several square miles of Torbay. The Tourist
Information Centres offer a great deal of helpful advice. Families
might well be interested to know that Paignton Zoo is a little way
along the ring road from Churston Ferrers.

Brixham, at the south eastern extremity of Torbay, is probably the most attractive of the built up areas. There is still an active fishing harbour at which William of Orange landed in 1688 on his way to accept the Crown. After his defeat at Waterloo in 1815 Napoleon stayed in the harbour on board *H.M.S. Bellerophon* prior to his final exile. The harbour is sheltered by the height of Berry Head, where a Napoleonic fort was superimposed on ancient earthworks. Much of the Head is now a country park, renowned for nesting coastal birds and unusual flora on the limestone rocks.

Brixham Museum includes the National Coastguard Museum, open during the summer season; there is also the British Fisheries Museum, open all the year round.

At Churston the 15th century church stands close to Churston Court, the village being an oasis of calm in this busy area. Close by is the Paignton and Dartmouth Steam Railway, one of the most attractive of the former British Rail closed down branch lines which have been renovated and re-opened by preservation groups.

Paignton & Kingswear Railway: GWR "Prairie" tank locomotive

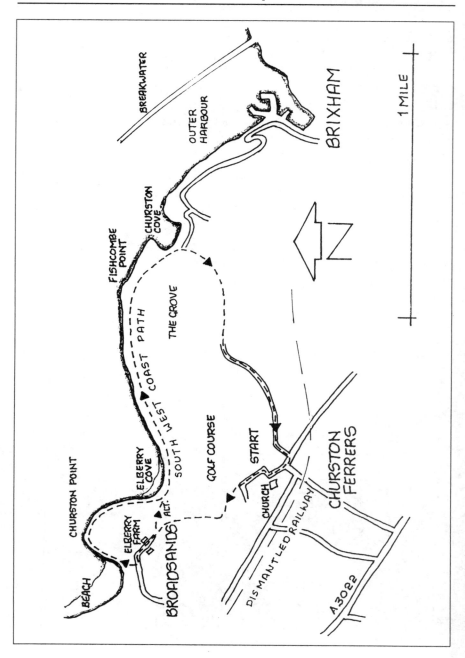

The Walk

From beside the church walk north to the sharp corner on the road. A track signposted "Broadsands" starts here. Pass Links Close and follow "footpath to the beach" to an old kissing gate.

Go across part of a golf course, keeping between the yellow posts. Enter woodland, ignore a stile on the right and proceed to another kissing gate. Turn right along a well used path close to houses, the nearest brush with suburbia on this walk. At a wide junction bear left for "Broadsands".

For the shorter version of the walk go right here.

Pass Elberry Farm and soon reach the car park, public conveniences and other attractions of Broadsands. Keep right, pass the beach huts and, at the far end of the sea wall, turn right at a "coast path – Elberry Cove" signpost, by a kissing gate.

Follow the South West Coast Path along the edge of the coast for fine walking on short grass, past a line of welcoming seats. There is plenty of opportunity to see much of the Torbay coastline as some height is gained. Fork left to descend to Elberry Cove and cross the back of the stony beach. *The shorter route re-joins the main route here.*

From the beach climb steeply through woodland. From the top the well worn path keeps close to the lower edge of the golf course and there are some opportunities for cliff top views along the way. On emerging from the trees the breakwater protecting Brixham harbour comes into sight and there is a steep descent to Churston Cove.

Don't take the first path on the right. Continue a little further to rise steeply through woods to a junction with a "Churston village" signpost. A wide path, later becoming a stony lane, rises slightly to pass through woods and meadows for more than one mile, so peaceful that it is difficult to realise that the holiday areas are so close on either hand. At the public road turn right, then right again at a junction to reach Ye Olde Churston Court, close to the car parking area.

21 Dartmouth

Length: 3¾ miles
Summary: This exhilarating walk has fine scenery along the South
West Coastal Path, the remains of Dartmouth castle,
St Petroc's church and an inland return route on good
paths and a lane across farming country.
Car Parking: National Trust car park at Little Dartmouth, accessed
from A379 near Stoke Fleming, grid reference 874492.
Map: Ordnance Survey Outdoor Leisure no. 20, South Devon
1:25,000 **or** Landranger no. 202, Torbay and South
Dartmoor, 1:50,000.

Tea Shop

Castle Tea Room – well worth entering this rather uninspiring
building. The interior is spotlessly clean and welcoming. From the
windows there are views of the castle and the estuary. Service is
extremely pleasant. Tempting snacks include a hot bacon bap,
toasties, pork and apple pasty, or strayed over the county border, a
Cornish pasty. For afternoon tea try the crumpets, or scones with
clotted cream and jam.

Open: 10.30am – 5pm every day from Easter to end of September.
Weekends only in October and during the autumn half-term holiday. If in any doubt please telephone **01803 833897**

Description

Although Dartmouth itself is not included within the itinerary of
this walk, it is very close and should certainly be visited for its
manifold attractions. Beautifully situated at the foot of steep slopes
close to the mouth of the estuary of the River Dart, the town has a
long and distinguished history, including participation in two crusades followed by centuries as one of the west country's leading
ports. The harbour entrance was defended by two castles on oppo-

Dartmouth Castle

site sides of the water – Dartmouth and Kingswear – which could be linked by a chain across the water in times of war, and by extra defences a little further upstream at Bayard's Cove.

As extra flat land was needed beside the river which was Dartmouth's life blood, shallow water has been filled; much of the present town is built on this reclaimed land. Despite this expansion the town is still squeezed between hillside and water, adding greatly to the charm of the narrow streets lined with fine old buildings, some being richly carved. The 17th century Butterwalk in Duke Street, now containing a small museum, is a particularly good example.

The mainly 14th century St Saviour's is the great church of Dartmouth, with a wealth of interesting features inside including a gallery and a particularly good screen.

Thomas Newcomen, producer of the first industrial steam engine, was born in Dartmouth, baptised here in 1663, and has a street named in his honour, together with a memorial in the public gardens.

High above the town is the hugely impressive "Brittania" Royal Naval College which was opened by King Edward VII at the outset of his reign, confirming Dartmouth's maritime importance.

Dartmouth castle dates from several periods of history and is now in the care of English Heritage. From April to October it is open to the public. Close by is St Petroc's (Petrox according to some writers) church, now mainly of the mid 17th century but with a Norman font and some early brasses.

The Walk

From the car park go through the kissing gate at the far end, heading for the sea along a good path (part of the south west coast path) at the edge of a large field. Go through another kissing gate behind Warren Cove, turning left to follow a broad inviting grassy track. The view behind includes the massive tower of Stoke Fleming church and, less appealingly, some visually obtrusive static caravans..

The track stays well above the sea, separated by a steeply dropping

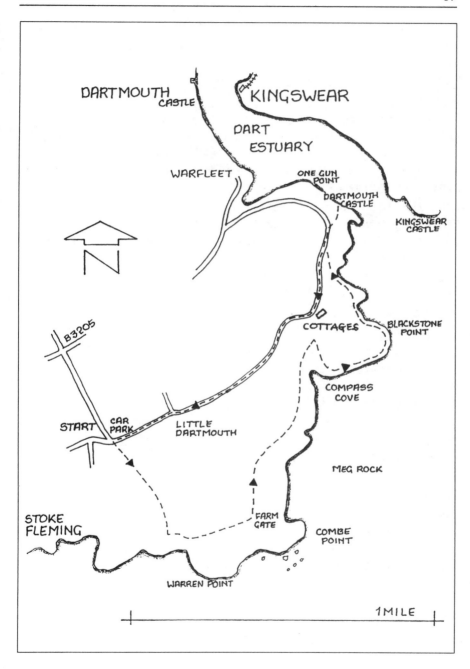

DARTMOUTH CASTLE

KINGSWEAR

DART ESTUARY

WARFLEET

ONE GUN POINT

DARTMOUTH CASTLE

KINGSWEAR CASTLE

B3205

COTTAGES

BLACKSTONE POINT

COMPASS COVE

START CAR PARK

LITTLE DARTMOUTH

MEG ROCK

STOKE FLEMING

FARM GATE

COMBE POINT

WARREN POINT

1MILE

gorse covered slope. Across the mouth of the Dart estuary the Mew Stone rises jaggedly from the water. By Coombe Point turn left at a farm gate with yellow arrow waymark. At a fork stay with the left, broader, track. Across the estuary the "tower" is prominent on high ground.

At the next junction ignore the stile on the left and continue to follow the south west coast path with the acorn waymark. In early March the first daffodils and primroses brighten the way along this most attractive of paths. The route goes downhill, with a sharp right bend as it returns towards the sea, soon reaching light woodland cladding the steep slope, with plenty of seats along the way.

At a surfaced roadway rise to a junction by a cottage and keep right towards Dartmouth Castle, signposted "Dartmouth 1 mile". In a few metres leave the roadway to take a path on the right through woodland, leading to the turning circle at the head of the castle's linear car park. Well below to the right is a large picnic area.

From the turning circle turn right, down steps, directly to the castle. There is a small "Dartmouth Castle and castle ferry" sign.

After refreshment and/or visits to the castle and St Petroc's church (there are also public conveniences), return up the path to the fork in the roadway. Follow the signpost "Little Dartmouth 1 mile" to ascend gently through the woodland, soon reaching Compass Cove Cottages, standing high with fine views out to sea.

An alternative ascent can be made by entering the National Trust access woodland on the right and climbing to a top stile before rejoining the road.

After the cottages go through a kissing gate into National Trust owned open countryside, then to a farm gate and grassy lane leading to the huge and not particularly attractive farmstead of Little Dartmouth. The way through the farm is obvious but there is a signpost "National Trust car park ¼ mile". Continue to the car park.

22. Torcross and Beesands

Length: 3½ miles

Summary: A circuit combining the villages of Torcross, Beesands and Beeson. The outward route is on lanes and footpaths, with a return along the South West Coastal Path over Torcross Point. The high ground between Torcross and Beesands is crossed in each direction.

Car Parking: Plenty of free car parking along the roadside at the back of the beach at Beesands. Typical grid reference 820406.

Map: Ordnance Survey Outdoor Leisure no. 20, South Devon, 1:25,000 **or** Landranger no. 202, Torbay and South Dartmoor, 1:50,000

Tea Shop

Sea Breeze Cottage, now a guest-house and tea shop, is over three hundred years old. The building has thick walls and a thatched roof and stands sturdily by the sea. The tea room is well appointed and most appealing. The photographs displayed on the walls depict the violent storms of 1979. For summer days there are tables outside in a sunny position overlooking the sea.

The extensive menu offers salads, sandwiches, including crab; toasted teacakes, plain teas, cream teas, cooked meals, and has a separate menu for children. Bed and breakfast is available in en-suite rooms. Open: 10.30am – 6pm (and sometimes later) every day from Easter to the end of October. Tel: 01548 580697

Description

Torcross is a small, generally unremarkable, seaside village squeezed between the watery expanse of Slapton Ley, the sea and the foot of the Torcross Point headland. The headland does little to protect Torcross from the occasional violent storms which batter

Torcross and Slapton Ley

this largely flat section of coastline. The recommended tea shop has some remarkable photographs of a storm in 1979.

Slapton Ley is a huge freshwater lake, now a Nature Reserve rich in water fowl, which has no visible outlet to the sea, the water percolating gently through the sand. This coast was used as an extensive training area for American forces prior to the 1944 Normandy landings. The whole countryside was evacuated, about 3,000 people having to leave their homes for a considerable period. Appreciation of this sacrifice was later shown by the erection of a monument by the U.S. government beside the coastal road half way along the Ley. By the car park in Torcross a Sherman tank, rescued from the sea, is another reminder of those difficult times.

As with Torcross, the site of Beesands as a linear village by the edge of the sea has resulted in periodic battering by storms. One bad storm each decade is apparently normal. The permitted excavation of half a million tons of shingle for the construction of Devonport dockyard at the turn of the century altered the natural configuration of the beach and is believed to be largely responsible for the dire

effect on Torcross, Beesands and the even more unfortunate Hall-
sands, which was entirely destroyed within twenty years of the
excavation. Nobody's favourite picture postcard seaside resort, Beesands has an uncared for, run down appearance. It does, however,
have an inn and public conveniences.

Beeson is a pleasant but unremarkable small village, half a mile
inland from Beesands.

The Walk

Follow the Beesands access road uphill, away from the sea. Bear
right at a junction, still rising, and continue to Beeson. Turn right
at the first road junction in the village, just past Riviera Cottage.
Before the next junction, by Lower Beeson Farm, turn right.

Take a waymarked track on the left a few metres further on, a
narrow lane rising steadily to Lower Widdicombe Farm. Bear right
at the farm. Take care here to find a footpath through a gate on the
left, immediately before a lane which beckons temptingly. The
signpost is partly concealed in the hedge.

The path goes up the right hand edge of a field to a waymarked
stile at the top. Keep to the same line to pass Widdicombe House.
Go over another stile in 50 metres and keep to the left of the House
access drive, soon entering pine woodland. Reach a tarmac track at
a signpost. Turn left for 20 metres, then right at a waymarked post
to a kissing gate.

Descend across a field to another kissing gate, to the left of an
obvious farm gate. The views include Mattiscombe Farm and Sto-
kenham village. Turn right along the minor road to reach Torcross.
The coastal views, encompassing Slapton Ley, are terrific, particularly from a viewpoint just before the final descent to Torcross.

The Sea Breeze tea room is found just a little way along the sea
front.

By the Village Inn, a flight of steps to the left is the start of the
official coast path back to Beesands. Should you wish to avoid these
steps, go to the right of the inn and start up the rising surfaced lane,
turning left in a short distance. The two routes come together by a

post with yellow arrows. Go past the front of the garage of a private house and turn right into a leafy track. There are more arrows to confirm the route.

Emerge into the open, with great views over Start Bay and to Start Point with its lighthouse. The well used track goes around the back of a long disused quarry. Soon, Beesands comes into view, with the pool of Widdicombe Ley in the foreground. Descend to the back of the shingle beach and walk back to the car parking.

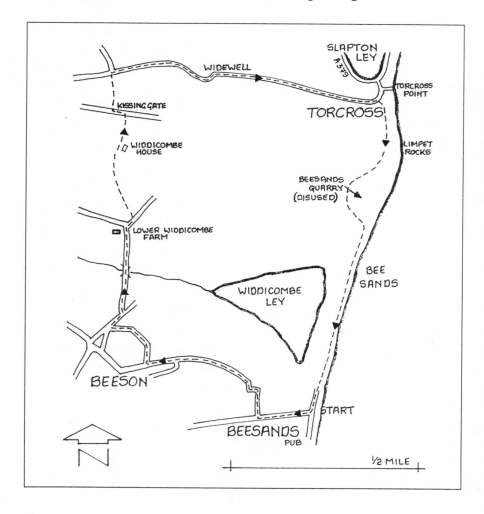

---

23. East Prawle

Length: 4 miles

Summary: A fine walk largely on the official South West Coast Path, with prime Devon coastal scenery including Prawle Point and Gammon Head. The ups and downs of the coast path are quite demanding and young children will require careful shepherding on some sections.

Car Parking: National Trust car park at end of cul de sac road, to the south from East Prawle village. Grid reference 775355

Map: Ordnance Survey Outdoor Leisure no. 20, South Devon, 1:25,000 **or** Landranger no. 202, Torbay and South Dartmoor, 1:50,000.

Tea Shop

"The Grunter" cannot be described as a typical "olde tea shoppe" by any stretch of the imagination! This tiny cafe seating around twenty is just across from the Pig's Nose Inn by The Green in East Prawle. The full menu, at very reasonable prices, is served all day. At ten o'clock many people were enjoying a "fry-up" breakfast. There was an aroma of good coffee and the background music was by Mozart. As well as the full breakfast, one may choose a bacon or sausage bap, sandwiches, salads, doughnuts, cakes, cream teas with home-made scones.

Open: 9.30am – 6pm from Easter to the end of September. Tel: 01548 511486

Description

East Prawle is situated a little way inland, high above the coastal cliffs. The village may not grace many picture post cards but, particularly out of high season, it has a wild, remote, feel which is not common along the South Devon coast. The curiously titled Pig's

Gammon Head near East Prawle

Nose Inn, the Grunter Tea Room and the Piglet shop are all grouped together in the village centre.

Only the Lizard and Land's End are further south than Prawle Point, which has a prominent former Lloyd's Signal Station, later used as a coastguard lookout. To the west is Gammon Head, separated from Prawle Point by a bay with a tiny but delectable sandy beach in a cove. Two ships from the Spanish Armada were wrecked on the fearsome rocks of this headland.

The Walk

From the car park turn left to descend to a gate and a signpost. Turn right to follow the coast path, with its characteristic acorn waymark, towards "Gara Rock 2½ miles".

Go uphill to the headland, with a detour to the left required to visit Prawle Point itself and the defunct coastguard lookout post. The fine view includes Bolt Head, more than 3 miles away on the far side of the Kingsbridge Estuary.

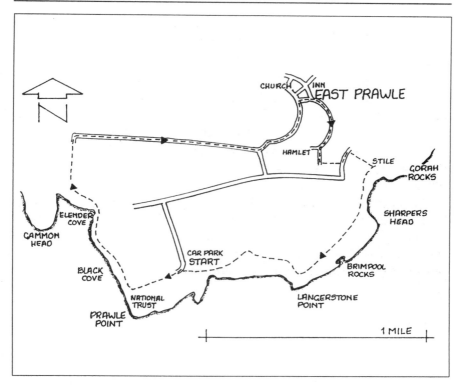

Continue along the path with the rusting hulk of a long ago shipwreck below. Gammon Head, seen across Ellender Cove, is most impressive along this section. Underfoot, some care is required and some parts of the path are rather exposed. By a little gem of a sandy beach there is a junction of paths, with yellow arrow waymarks. Go up to the right here and, in a few metres, at another waymarked post go left.

A well used track climbs steadily inland for about a quarter of a mile. At a junction waymarked with blue and yellow arrows turn right. A typically Devon unsurfaced lane goes almost straight and almost level for the best part of a mile, with occasional fine views on the seaward side.

Join a surfaced road and turn left to reach East Prawle village, with public conveniences, inn, tea room and shop. Continue along the cul de sac road opposite the entrance to Grunter's Tea Room, soon downhill. At an outlying hamlet fork left on to an unsurfaced lane, signposted "public bridleway Gorah Rocks ½ mile"

In 150 metres or so turn left over a waymarked stile to follow a faint field path descending steeply. This route cuts off a corner and has the extra reward of superb coastal views. At the bottom go through a gate and negotiate a rather awkward drop into the lane below. Turn left to reach a gate in a few metres. Fork right here for another short cut along the edge of a cornfield to reach the coast path.

Turn right over a stile and follow this path, here easy and almost level, all the way back to the signpost below the car park. Turn right to return. This section of the coast is quite unusual in that the former sea cliffs are so set back that there is space for tiny cultivated fields (and a good path) between them and the sea.

24. Sharpitor (Salcombe)

Length: 4½ miles

Summary: Bolt Head, Sharp Tor and the National Trust property of
Overbecks Museum and garden are all included to
give a particularly fine walk close to Salcombe. Whilst
enthusiasts will claim, with reason, that the South West
Coast Path is never really dull, no one could dispute
that the section included in this walk is one of the very
finest. The rise and fall is no more than average and
the going is first rate throughout.

Car Parking: Free car parking area in a remote situation at the end of
a cul de sac road beyond Higher Soar Farm. Accessed
from Malborough by heading west from the village,
passing the church, forking left and then heading south
towards the various Soar farms for about two miles.
Grid reference 713375.

Map: Ordnance Survey Outdoor Leisure no. 20, South Devon,
1:25,000 **or** Landranger no. 202, Torbay and South
Dartmoor, 1:50,000.

Tea Shop

The tea facility at Overbecks (National Trust) is unique; during the
afternoon refreshments are available to visitors to the museum and
gardens. At other times it becomes the dining room for the Youth
Hostel. The atmosphere, whilst quite acceptable, is bordering on the
institutional with one large room with big solid tables and matching
chairs. The somewhat restricted menu includes soup and rolls,
cakes, Salcombe hand-made biscuits, tea, coffee, cold drinks, and
ice cream.

Open: Easter or 1st April – end of October: 12 noon – 4.15pm;
closed on Saturdays Tel: 01548 843238

Sea cliffs and coast path near Salcombe

Description

At Sharpitor on the southern fringe of Salcombe, Overbecks House and garden is managed by the National Trust. The mild climate encourages a rich growth of many rare and tender plants. The Edwardian house does an unusual double duty as museum with tea room and youth hostel. From 1st April to the end of October the museum is open daily, apart from Saturdays, from 11.00am to 5.00pm. The garden is open throughout the year from 10.00am until 8.00pm (or sunset if earlier).

Bolt Head, Starehole Bay, Sharp Tor and the Kingsbridge estuary provide an altogether beautiful accompaniment to the attraction of this property.

Although not included in the route, Salcombe is so close that a visit is likely to be combined with the walk. The mild climate has undoubtedly contributed to the great popularity of this boating and holiday resort. The local history museum at Custom House Quay includes exhibits portraying the town's history as a port of moderate importance. There are two good sand beaches between Sharpitor and the town proper.

The Walk

Head down the surfaced track pointing towards the sea, soon reaching what appears to be a small abandoned wartime building. Turn right in a few metres to take a footpath signposted "link to coast path". An obvious path crosses a meadow, aiming just to the left of the sad looking abandoned buildings of Middle Soar Farm.

Pass the farm and continue to a gate with a signpost on the far side. Turn left to "Bolt Head ¾ mile". The path is over close cropped grass close to a wall on the left. Bolt Head is soon in view ahead. Just before a gate/stile the South West Coast Path is joined. Go over the stile and walk across a field to a choice of route. *To include Bolt Head go through the kissing gate on the right, rise to the Head and then bend left to descend to Starehole Bottom.*

To by-pass the Head keep left, following the "Starehole Bottom" signpost. This avoiding path goes straight on before slanting left

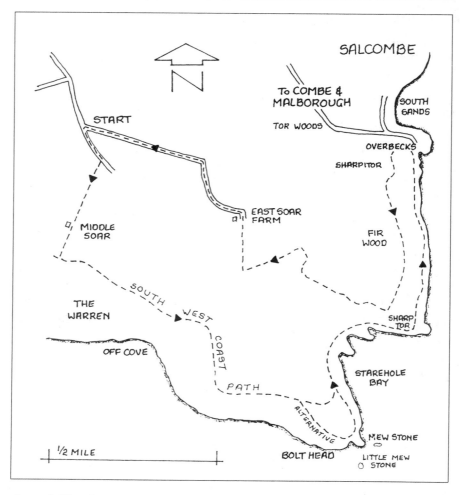

downhill. There are more gates and signposts on the way to the junction with the coast path just behind the bay. Turn left and enjoy a wonderful section of the coast path as it squeezes its improbable way between Sharp Tor and the sea, with fine views all the way.

Go through a wood and pass a house to reach an unsurfaced roadway. Rise to join a surfaced road and turn left for a steady climb to the entrance to Overbecks, with tea room, museum and gardens.

Exit from Overbecks and turn left at a track with a National Trust

Bolt Head sign and "Sharp Tor. Upper Cliff Path" The stony track rises along the side of the gardens. Soon there is ample reward for the effort expended, with superb views up and across the estuary. Pass a trig. point on the right and continue to Sharp Tor, which has an orientation table. On a clear day places far and near are visible; across the estuary is Prawle Point, with the abandoned coastguard station.

The track now swings to the right among vast swathes of gorse. Starehole Cove is below to the left; ahead is East Soar Farm. Care in route finding is needed as an isolated farm building is approached. At a junction of paths turn right, over a stile, signposted "Soar Mill Cove". Go up the field over grass to another signpost in 100 metres. Continue the same line aiming for a gate to the right hand side of the farm.

Go through and pass the farm complex on a stony track, the route confirmed by yellow arrows on posts. After another gate an unsurfaced roadway provides a good level tramp unerringly back to the car park, with a sharp left bend part way along. To the right is a small airfield and, beyond, the village of Malborough is visible.

25. Loddiswell and the Avon Valley

Length: 3½ miles

Summary: An attractive circuit with much of interest in this quiet part of the valley of England's fourth River Avon. A steep climb up the valley side after refreshments and some mud, but otherwise very easy walking.

Car Parking: Small car park with public conveniences in Loddiswell village, signposted from the main road. Grid reference 719486,

Map: Ordnance Survey Outdoor Leisure no. 20, South Devon, 1:25,000 **or** Landranger no. 202, Torbay and South Dartmoor, 1:50,000.

Tea Shop

"The Station Platform" is the pride and joy of Sheila Hall and Harry Moss. They live in the old station and greatly enjoy meeting people, sharing their enthusiasm for the former railway line, and even more

importantly serving award winning cream teas in this peaceful and unusual setting. Don't miss visiting Loddiswell station but try to choose a fine day as there is no indoor accommodation. However the platform is very sheltered so it isn't very often a problem. Teas only but

Sheila will serve any combination – with cream or without, and even allow one tea between two if customers wish to preserve some appetite for dinner!

Open: hours are somewhat restricted and are normally from Easter to October during weekends and school holidays only – 2 – 5.30pm but could vary. Try telephoning first. Tel: 01548 550462

As an alternative, refreshments can be taken at The Avon Mill Garden Centre – refer to walk below.

Description

High on a hillside above the River Avon, three miles north of Kingsbridge, Loddiswell village straddles the road to California Cross. Despite its modest size the village does have an inn, post office stores and the parish church of St Michael and All Angels, basically 14th century but with 15th century extensions.

From a junction with the Great Western Railway west country main line at South Brent, a branch railway line was constructed to Kingsbridge. Although this had been proposed as early as 1861, it was not until 1893 that the line was constructed and opened. For the greater part of its length the line follows the Avon valley, with the result that the station serving Loddiswell was three-quarters of a mile from the village, along a lane descending steeply for more than 200 feet. As with so many scenic but unprofitable lines, closure in 1963 followed publication of the Beeching report.

The Walk

Leave the car park by turning left. Turn left again to pass the post office/stores and then the parish church by a lane between stone walls. After the church continue along the surfaced road. At the Ham Butts junction continue towards "Reads Farm ½" on a lane down the side of the Avon valley.

By the entrance to Reads Farm turn right at a signposted gate to follow a defined path which skirts round the farm. Go over a stile and continue, accompanied by a small stream on the left. The route is well wooded and a yellow arrow points the way towards a possibly muddy sunken section of the path and a small bridge over the stream. Turn left to cross and head for the river, where a finger post directs to the left.

Continue by the side of the river, the path soon becoming better defined. The banks are richly wooded, sycamore, ash and holly all being present. On the left of the path a former mill leat of considerable size is soon apparent. By a blown over tree go over a stile but don't be tempted to use the suspended rope as a potential short cut across the river!

Cross a bridge over the leat and continue the same line. At the point where the leat takes its water, a long weir still crosses the river. After another stile and a bridge reach a sunken lane and turn right. Here is a fine skewed double arch bridge by which the railway crossed the river.

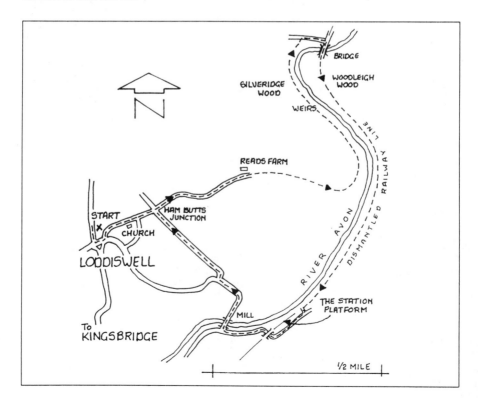

Cross the bridge and follow the former railway trackbed for almost one mile, in a deep cutting for a short distance. The line runs through Woodleigh Wood, which is in the care of the Woodland Trust. As the former Loddiswell station is approached, there is a notice pointing out that this route is permitted but is not a right of way. Accordingly it is closed on the first Monday of each January. Should you wish to walk on that day, a footpath close to the former line provides a good alternative.

By the notice turn left over a stile, then right to pass the station. A few surviving railway buildings will be of interest to the enthusiast. Go over a stile and turn right for access to the tea room on the former platform of the station.

Leave the station by turning right, downhill, at the public road. Go under another fine bridge and turn right at the first junction. Cross the river to reach Avon Mill, now a garden centre with refreshment facilities (open Monday to Saturday except Tuesdays 10.30am to 5pm Sunday 2pm to 5pm)

Continue past the mill, the road now rising steeply. As the road bends left and the gradient eases turn right into an unmade lane, then left in 40 metres. This track rises at a steady gradient to the junction at Ham Butts. Turn left to return to Loddiswell village and the car park.

26. Aveton Gifford

Length: 4½ miles
Summary: A very varied walk indeed combining the estuary of the
                   River Avon with farming upland, using minor roads,
                   unsurfaced lanes and field paths. The full circuit has
                   some rough walking sections where rights of way are ill
                   defined. Plenty of ups and downs.
Car Parking: Sizeable free car park with information board by the
                   roundabout at the south end of Aveton Gifford. Grid
                   reference 693473.
Map: Ordnance Survey Outdoor Leisure no. 20, South Devon,
                   1:25,000 **or** Landranger no. 202, Torbay and South
                   Dartmoor, 1:50,000.

Tea Shop

The Balkwill family run Court Barton Farm, which is beautifully
and quietly situated above the village and near to the church. Jill
Balkwill provides bed and breakfast accommodation and farmhouse teas are served either inside the house or in the garden. The
menu offers purely afternoon tea – cream tea, plain tea, fruit cake,
flapjacks, ice cream, coffee, tea, and cold drinks.

Open: 2pm – 6pm, Easter to the end of June – weekends only. In
the main summer months, every day. Advisable to check if in any
doubt. Tel. 01548 550312

Description

The upper portion of the estuary of England's fourth River Avon is
a pleasantly quiet area, much nicer than the seaward end which is
marred by the nondescript development at Bigbury on Sea.

Now by-passed by the main A79 road, Aveton Gifford is a relatively quiet village. Although there are plenty of good old buildings,
it has never become a showpiece or a tourist honeypot. At the north

Estuary of the River Avon

east end of the village, near the tea rooms, the late 13th century parish church of St Andrew was almost totally destroyed by enemy action during World War II. It does seem to be an unlikely target! The church was originally of cruciform shape, with central tower and access through a round turret on the south side. The fine porch on the north side escaped damage. The church was re-consecrated in 1957 after rebuilding by a local firm, old stonework and modern construction being exceptionally well blended.

Just to the south of the car park, the old Aveton Gifford bridge spans the River Avon.

The Walk

Turn right at the bottom of the car park on to a minor road along the side of the estuary, soon reaching a ford. If the tide is out continue along the road. Otherwise, divert to the right along a signposted footpath then turn left to cross a stream and return to the estuarial road. For about half a mile the little road makes an enjoyable walking route beside the tidal water.

Just before reaching the next ford turn right at a public footpath
signpost. A delightful path under overhanging trees follows the tidal
portion of a tributary stream. Slant up to a stile as the path dimin-
ishes and rise through woodland. Join a wider path and keep left,
passing lush wetland vegetation below to the left.

Turn right at a minor road and, in less than 200 metres, turn right
into a gravely lane, rising quite steeply. The lane is obviously used
as a bridleway but is a little overgrown near the top. There are long
views from a gate at the top. Bear right here over a stile with yellow
arrow, near a cattle grid.

The path is not well defined; follow the hedge and then bear right
to another stile. As a large cultivated field is crossed the views are
very fine, the path being just about visible as it descends roughly in
line with a minor road which heads for the main road ahead. Keep
well to the left of a small wooded area with a low farm building. Go
over the stile in the bottom corner. *(If you don't like crossing large
cultivated fields, you could stay with the lane and turn right at a minor
road to descend to Waterhead Bridge).*

Turn left at the very minor road, pass the front of a house at
Waterhead Bridge and turn sharp right at another road. In 20 metres
turn sharp left at a public footpath sign.

*(Shorter version – do not turn left as above, but follow the minor
road to its junction with the main road. Go straight across and head
for the church. The Court Barton Tea Rooms are just before the lych
gate)*

Go through a gate and along the bottom of a sloping field. The
path becomes rather vague. Go over the arrowed stile at the next
fence. From this stile the right of way goes to the far fence and then
turns left, very steeply uphill. A diagonal line would be a much
easier way of reaching the next stile, which is almost at the top of
the field.

After this stile bend left then right to keep above the grounds of
Ashford Mill, along the bottom of a field. After the next stile angle
down the slope of the field over rough ground, aiming for a stile in
the bottom boundary, just over half way along. Go over the stile and

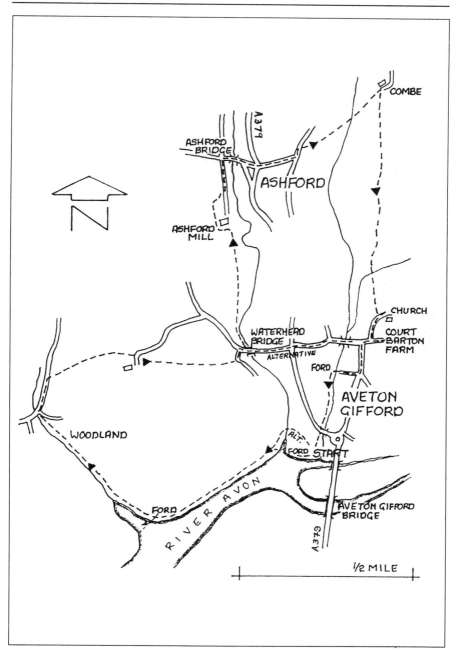

turn left along a good track. Turn right at the public road, cross Ashford bridge, pass Ashford farm house and fork left at a junction.

Rise to the main road and cross over into a semi-surfaced lane, still rising. Go left at a junction. In another 40 metres go through a gate on the right, with a "public bridleway" sign. The way stays close to the hedge on the left for some distance, with good open views to Aveton Gifford and beyond. Do not go through the hedge at a tempting gap but keep right to cross a stream and reach a gate.

A good path now rises towards Combe After another gate turn right at a "public bridleway" sign. The track rises towards another similar sign but, before that sign, turn right to follow an obvious path along the valley side, parallel with the stream. This path starts well but the next field is cultivated and the path goes straight ahead to cross a tributary valley at a waymarked stone stile and sleeper bridge.

Follow the indicated line through more rough country then along the bottom edge of a cultivated field to another stile and sleeper bridge, then across another field to yet another stile. Angle left up a grass slope to a rudimentary gate and bear right to the village. At the public road turn right, then left at Pulley's Corner to go to the tea rooms and/or the church.

To return, descend to the main street at Tree Corner and turn left. There is now a choice between walking down the village street **or** turning right at Jubilee Street and then left by a mini ford to continue across playing fields. Descend a few steps and follow the stream to the Fishermen's Rest Inn. Take the pedestrian tunnel under the by-pass, directly to the car park.

27. Wembury

Length: 3¼ miles

Summary: An easy and straightforward walk using a section of the
South West Coast Path close to the estuary of the
River Yealm, not far from Plymouth.

Car Parking: National Trust car park by Wembury beach (members
free, non-members pay). Grid reference 517484. **or** by
the entrance to the nearby church (if there is no
function at the church).

Map: Ordnance Survey Outdoor Leisure no. 20, South Devon,
1:25,000 **or** Landranger no. 201, Plymouth and
Launceston, 1:50,000.

Tea Shop

The beautifully-situated tea shop at Wembury Mill is tiny and cosy.
The menu offers sandwiches, savouries such as "hot dogs", toasted
teacakes, cream teas, milk-shakes, and ice cream.

Open: 10.30am – 5pm from Easter or 1st April to end of October.
Tel: 01752 862314

Description

Wembury is a large village of generally suburban character with
little of interest in the village itself. However, by the edge of the sea,
detached from the village proper, is a high standing church with a
former mill at the back of the beach below, making an attractive little
area. The church is dedicated to the Saxon St Werbergh and according to legend this is the site of a Saxon settlement, a great battle being
fought here against invading Danes about 1,000 years ago.

Although restored in the 19th century, the church still has some
15th century and possibly earlier work. Inside is a great monument
to Sir John Hele who died in 1608. As Sergeant at Law he took part
in the trial of Sir Walter Raleigh.

The Old Mill Tea Shop

The former mill is now in the care of the National Trust and is used as a seasonal cafe (see Tea Shop, above), The estuary of the River Yealm may be crossed by a foot ferry from Warren Point to Noss Mayo.

The Walk

Start up the steep path behind the National Trust car park, heading to the right of the church *(from the church car park there is a connecting path across the churchyard)*. In 100 metres or so turn left at a yellow arrowed post and pass through a kissing gate, close to the end of the church.

A grassy track rises along the edge of a meadow. The views behind, over the church to the Great Mew Stone, are splendid. The path continues through another kissing gate. At a lane turn left, then almost immediately right at a waymarked path to follow "public footpath Brownhill Lane". Go over a stile and note the warning about feeding the horses!

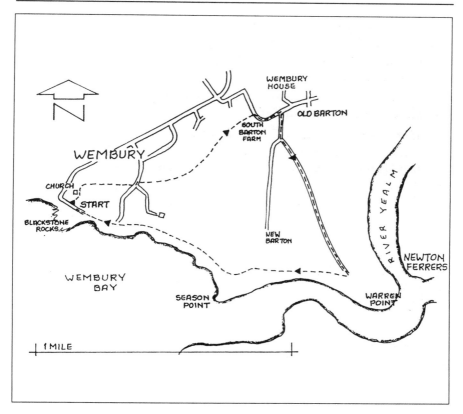

The track goes diagonally across a field to a kissing gate in the corner. Bear left along the side of the hedge in the next field to another kissing gate, then along the edge of a cultivated field. Soon the path skirts the fringe of residential Wembury, before passing South Barton Farm. Go through a kissing gate to an unmade lane, and turn right along the lane, soon bearing left to reach a surfaced road.

Turn sharp right at a signpost "public footpath 26 – to coastal path". The track soon loses its surface. Go straight across at a junction, heading for "ferry and coastal path". Part way along this gently descending straightforward route, Newton Ferrers comes into sight across the estuary of the River Yealm and the sea and estuarial views open up splendidly.

At a gate enter the National Trust owned Warren Point land. At a stone "left – view of River Yealm, right – Wembury", turn right to take the South West Coast Path. This is a relatively level section of the path, easy walking, and with views across Wembury Bay to H.M.S. Cambridge, a shore based establishment on the far headland. Just inland is New Barton Farm.

In less than half a mile a diversion to the left is to Season Point. Stay with the coast path at any intersection, eventually descending to the National Trust car park and the distinctive mill tea shop below.

28. Buckland Abbey

Length: 3 miles (shorter options available)

Summary: A walk to be combined with a visit to this former Abbey. For the most part fairly level, using field and woodland paths. There may be some mud during and after wet weather. Free admission for members of the National Trust who now look after the Abbey; entrance fee for non-members.

Car Parking: At the Abbey, well signposted from the Yelverton direction. Yelverton is two miles to the east, Plymouth nine miles to the south. Grid reference 490667.

Map: Ordnance Survey Outdoor Leisure no. 28, Dartmoor (just about!), 1:25,000 **or** Landranger no. 201, Plymouth and Launceston, 1:50,000.

Tea Shop

The large tea room at Buckland Abbey is very much in character with its ecclesiastical origins; the decor echoes a monastic refectory. However the menu is certainly not that of a restrictive order and a most pleasant afternoon tea can be enjoyed.

The filter coffee is excellent; there is a good choice of blends of tea as well as fruit infusions. Cold drinks include organic English apple juice and home-made orange or lemon squash. Lunches, cream teas, home-made cakes, are all of good quality. Friendly service. Fresh flowers on each table add to the welcoming environment. Open: Easter or 1st April 10.30 – 5pm daily but closed on Thursdays. Other months, open on Saturdays and Sundays from 12.30 – 5pm. Tel. – 01822 855024

Description

The Abbey is very much the focal point of this walk. Founded in 1278 by Cistercian monks, it was dissolved by Henry VIII in 1539. The Grenville family became owners, most of the buildings being converted into a fine country house. Grandson of the original Grenville owner was Sir Richard Grenville of "Revenge" fame. Sea-faring ownership was continued when Sir Francis Drake acquired the house in 1581. It remained his home during the troubled years of the war with Spain and the arrival of the Armada. The Drake family continued in occupation until comparatively recent times.

Since 1951 in the care of the National Trust and well restored, the Abbey now offers visitors a wealth of interesting rooms and exhibits which include the (somewhat dubious?) Drake's Drum. The grounds are extensive and beautiful and the Great Barn is one of the largest in the country.

The Walk

Choose one of the four colour coded and waymarked trails set out in the leaflet available at the Abbey reception. Both "blue" and "red" walks extend to about 3 miles and include part of Great North Wood in the valley of the nearby River Tavy. Those with less time or energy will prefer the "yellow" walk of three-quarters of a mile, largely on hard pathway. All walks include both woodland and open farming country.

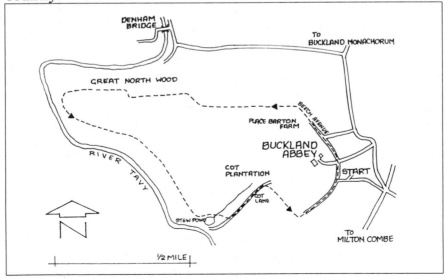

29. Burrator and the Meavy Valley

Length: 5½ miles

Summary: A well varied and attractive circuit with something of
interest for everybody. Included are a disused railway
line, the historic Devonport water supply leat, a relict
industrial landscape, prehistoric remains and forest. All
this and a farm tea shop too!

Car Parking: Free car parking at Norsworthy Bridge at the far end of
Burrator Reservoir, reached along the road from
Dousland. Grid reference 568694.

Map: Ordnance Survey Outdoor Leisure no. 28, Dartmoor,
1:25,000 **or** Landranger no. 202, Torbay and South
Dartmoor, 1:50,000.

Tea Shop

The atmosphere at Peek Hill Farm is relaxed and friendly. Justine
Colton appears to take everything very placidly. Surrounded by her
children, she chats amiably to visitors, hires out bikes with advise
on routes, and serves teas! The farm is a working Dartmoor Farm so
the visit is interesting quite apart from the need for refreshments.
Limited menu – cream teas, coffee, cold drinks, and ice cream.

Open: at Easter and Bank Holidays and each day during July,
August, and September from 2 – 6pm. Worth trying at anytime – if
in doubt, do telephone first. Tel: 01822 854808

Description

By general agreement, the 1½ mile long Burrator Reservoir is much
the finest lake in the Dartmoor National Park, its tree fringed shores
having been likened to those of a Scottish loch. To the north of the
reservoir the boulder strewn heights of Leather Tor and Sharpitor
are dominant, their summits providing bird's eye views of the

reservoir and over a wide expanse of surrounding countryside. East of the reservoir Sheep's Tor is similarly impressive.

The reservoir was first opened in 1898 to supply the needs of Plymouth for a copious supply of good quality water. During the 1920s the level was raised by 3 metres to increase the overall capacity. There are two dams at the south end. There is an encircling road and visitors to this fine area have been encouraged by the provision of car parking areas at each end, forest trails, and the construction of public conveniences.

Devonport Leat aqueduct over the River Meavy

The Devonport leat superseded Drake's leat in 1793, supplying water to Plymouth and Devonport until the opening of Burrator Reservoir. It collects water from sources high on the moor and transports it for many winding miles, generally descending at very gentle gradients. Close to the aqueduct over the River Meavy it does, however, rush furiously down a steep hillside.

The Yelverton to Plymouth branch railway line, which is featured in this walk, is described in Walk no. 30.

The Walk

Head directly away from Norsworthy Bridge up a broad, stony track with several colours of waymarking. Bear left in about 50 metres. Before the valley was flooded Norsworthy Farm stood at this place. The river is rushing along below on the left, with some mining remains to be seen on its banks. Ignore the numerous stiles and side paths and keep to the wide track rising through mixed woodland.

Leather Tor Bridge, a massive 19th century clapper, is soon reached. Do not cross but continue along the same track, forking left in 50 metres. Ahead are Hart Tor and the TV mast on North Hessary Tor. Go over a stile to reach more open country and continue up the Meavy valley, here very much a relict landscape, re-shaped by the waste heaps of the former tin mining.

The line of the path is by no means always obvious as it weaves about among the heaps and the bracken, never far from the infant River Meavy. Behind, Leather Tor rises superbly over the conifer forest. In less than half a mile the aqueduct which carries the Devonport leat over the river is reached. Climb up the damaged stone facade or, perhaps preferably, veer a little to the right for an easier ascent to the base of the fine rushing cascade. Cross the aqueduct and follow the leat round to the left for almost half a mile. The right bank has a good path.

As the leat bends left on a low embankment, about 200 metres before entering the conifer woodland, bear right. Cross a small stream and rise across grass to the start of an obvious track, a grassy swathe through the bracken. Continue to rise to the top corner of

the wall enclosing the plantation, then the main Yelverton to Princetown road. Leather Tor and Sharpitor dominate the view on this
ascent.

Turn left and walk by the roadside for about half a mile. Pass a
car park and go uphill. The former railway line is visible to the right
as it makes its huge detour around King's Tor (walk no. 30). At the
top of the hill is another car park, a small pond and a stone row.
From this point our route follows a right of way marked on the

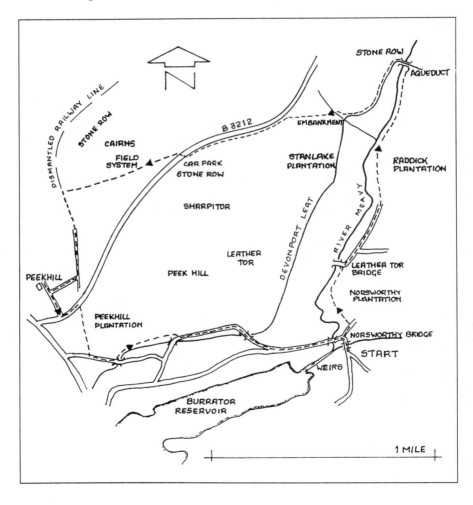

Ordnance Survey map forking right at an angle of 30 degrees or so to the road. On the ground there appears to be no positive path but several possible semi paths. The going is perfectly easy underfoot and a line aiming a little to the left of the prominent church above Walkhampton is about right.

The former railway line is reached at a dismantled bridge. Go through a gate to the left of the bridge, marked "footpath" and turn left through another gate along the former track bed. In just under half a mile a stile is reached, hopefully adorned with a "Farm House Cream Teas" notice. Do not go over but turn right along a tiny lane to head for Peek Hill Farm.

Leave the farm by the surfaced access road, rising to the main road. Turn left for 80 metres, to the obvious railway line and turn right over a stile to take the "permitted path". Climb to the embankment, a fine viewpoint, and continue along the former trackbed, soon between areas of woodland. Turn left at a minor road, passing newly planted trees. In about a quarter of a mile the Devonport leat can be seen on the right.

Turn left here up a flight of steps to a stile and bear right to follow a grassy path by the leat. There are yellow waymarks along the way, which soon becomes a wide track through the conifers. Go over a rather awkward stone stile to reach more open country and a signboard by a bridge over the by now very familiar Devonport leat. The extensive views include Sheep's Tor and part of the reservoir with the dam at the far end.

Go ahead to follow "Stanlake Farm", soon rejoining the minor road. Turn left, again beside the Devonport leat. The road is very quiet, with a grass verge, dipping to the right to cross the leat. In 20 metres there is an old cross on the right, at Cross Gate. Join the lakeside road and turn left to return over the bridge to the parking place.

30. Princetown

Length: 5 miles

Summary: A circuit for those who enjoy wide open spaces. For tea shop walkers a relatively rare opportunity to sample the wildness of the open moorland. Interest is added by the remains of tin mining, quarrying and the former Princetown branch railway line. Rise and fall are only moderate and there are no problems underfoot.

Car Parking: Roadside car park on the Tavistock to Two Bridges road (B3357) at the junction with the access roadway to Yellowsmeade Farm. Grid reference 568749.

Map: Ordnance Survey Outdoor Leisure no. 28, Dartmoor, 1:25,000 **or** Landranger no. 191, Okehampton and North Dartmoor area, 1:50,000.

Tea Shop

The Mother Earth Tea Room, a new venture, was opened at the end of 1995 by Veronica Court. She makes all the cakes, and also the soup – a cauldron is always at the ready and sometimes very welcome indeed, for the weather can be poor even in summer in this desolate part of Devon. Hot pies, pasties, toasted sandwiches, and cream teas are also served.

Open: Mon – Fri, 10am – 5pm; Sat 9am – 7.30pm; Sun 9am – 6pm; every day all the year except Christmas Day. Tel: 01822 890204

Description

Claimed to be the highest town in England, it comes as no surprise to find that Princetown is a desolate, windswept place. The dominance of the 19th century prison buildings inevitably adds to the overall grimness.

The history of the town really started with the construction of the prison by French prisoners of war, starting in 1806. The already large number of Napoleonic war prisoners was enhanced by an influx of Americans in 1812, rising to an eventual total of about 7,000 men. Before 1806 there was little more than the Plume of Feathers Inn at this remote spot. The prisoners were paid to build the church (1810 -14) and other buildings followed.

The land is owned by the Duchy of Cornwall, the town being named after the then Prince of Wales and Duke of Cornwall, later crowned as King George IV. The rapid growth of Princetown and the siting here of the prison were due to the initiative of Sir Edward Tyrwhitt, a steward of the Duchy.

After the end of the wars the prison closed in 1816 and to maintain Princetown as a viable community Tyrwhitt introduced various agricultural and mineral enterprises on the surrounding parts of the moor. Not surprisingly in such a harsh environment the agricultural enterprises failed, but minerals were a different story. A 24 mile long horse drawn tramway was opened in 1823 linking Sutton harbour, Plymouth with Princetown. Coal, lime, sea sand and general merchandise were brought up to the moor and large quantities of stone were taken in return. The line was later partly converted to standard gauge and the part over Dartmoor became the Yelverton to Princetown branch of the Great Western Railway, winding sinuously around King's Tor in its struggle to reach 420 metres (nearly 1,400 feet). As the quarry trade waned, such an unlikely passenger carrying lane could not possibly survive and was closed in 1956. The trackbed now facilitates good upland walking.

Continued survival for Princetown was guaranteed in 1850 when the prison was re-opened as a civil institution, arguably the best known in the country. Horror tales of escaped prisoners perishing miserably in the bogs and mists of miles and miles of desolate moorland have flourished greatly in the ensuing years. In a similar vein, without unduly stretching the imagination, on a misty day one can hear the deep baying of Conan Doyle's Baskerville hound as it roams eternally over these interminable hillsides.

Modern Princetown does try to encourage visitors, with a nearly new heritage and information centre opened by the present Duke of Cornwall, Prince Charles, and with varied refreshment opportuni-

ties. There is also a museum housed in the former waterworks
building of the prison, open from April to September, Tuesday –
Saturday and Bank Holidays, 9.30am to 4.30pm; October – March,
Tuesday to Saturday, 9.30am to 12.30pm and 1.30pm to 4pm. The
museum is signposted and has its own car park. Opening may be
subject to prison operational requirements and visitors are warned
to lock their cars!

The Walk

Turn left along the stony roadway leading to Yellowmeade Farm.
On the right are some curious, obviously industrial, remains – long,
narrow enclosures with stone pillared entrances at the near ends.
Nearby is a solitary wind battered yew tree. Those who like to
identify the many and various Dartmoor tors will be pleased to name
a wide range from the vantage point of this high track. The line of
the former railway on the side of King's Tor shows up particularly
well.

Yellowmeade Farm

Fork left to pass above the farm, surely a strong candidate in any contest to find the most desolate habitation in Devon. As the track continues to the disused Foggintor quarries, note the granite blocks which held the rails of an early tramway. Pass the quarry, which still has a few ruined buildings.

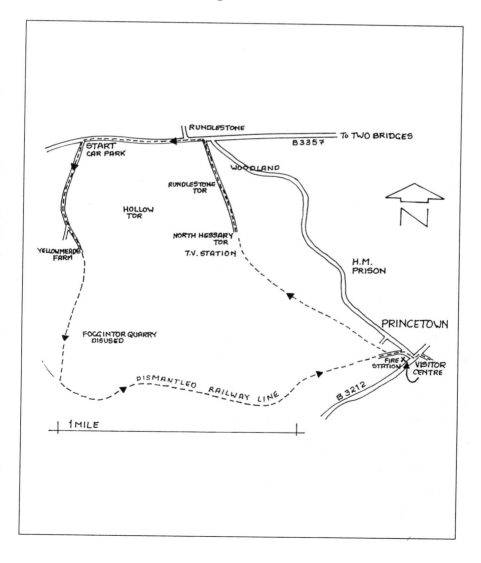

Beyond the quarry the track joins the trackbed of the former railway line. Turn left to walk towards Princetown, almost two miles distant from this point. All traces of line, sleepers etc. have been removed, but note the severity of the gradients and curves and imagine the sharp "bark" of the exhaust as the sweating fireman laboured whilst the driver coaxed his G.W.R. "prairie" tank up this difficult line.

After passing ground much disturbed by tin mining, a section by a tree plantation is the only part of the whole walk from which the TV/radio mast on North Hessary Tor is not visible. Fork left at the approach to Princetown, pass the fire station and turn right to reach Mother Earth, opposite the visitor centre.

Start the return walk along the road towards the fire station. Turn right at a public footpath sign opposite the fire station, then left at a surfaced road and head for the mast on North Hessary Tor, passing a small housing estate. Take a stony track to a gate, with various "Tyrwhitt Trails" notices.

The way up North Hessary Tor is never in doubt, a steady but not too severe climb directly to the TV station. There is evidence of former tin mining to the left of the route. The Tor has a height of 517 metres (almost 1,700 feet) and the top of the mast is the highest point in the southern half of Britain. There is a rocky summit but it is a mere pimple on the surface of this great mound.

The route continues along the TV station access road, although the Ordnance Survey does show a line distinctly to the left of the road, passing over Rundlestone Tor. The road is certainly easier and more straightforward, particularly as the public road is approached and the indicated path across a few small fields is difficult to identify.

Away to the left is Hollow Tor; ahead, at a distance, is Great Mis Tor. Turn left at the road to return to the car park, passing a house named Wheal Lucky, presumably a name derived from nearby tin mining.

TEA SHOP WALKS... *Spreading everywhere!*

Join in the fun ... explore the most scenic parts of Britain with these attractive, reliable walking guides. Each one features easy walks, wonderful scenery, plus plenty of background information to add interest – and naturally they all include teashops that welcome walkers!

TEA SHOP WALKS *in the* CHILTERNS

Jean Patefield

SIGMA *Leisure*

A SHOP WALKS *in* CHESHIRE

Clive Price

SIGMA *Leisure*

A SHOP WALKS *in the* PEAK DISTRICT

Norman & June Buckley

SIGMA *Leisure*

The 'tea shop' range already covers these attractive areas: Lake District • Lancashire • Cheshire • Cotswolds • Peak District • Shropshire • Surrey & Sussex • Yorkshire Dales – with many more to come – Great value books at £6.95 each

MORE COUNTRY WALKS:

LAKELAND ROCKY RAMBLES: Geology beneath your feet – Bryan Lynas (£9.95)

LAKELAND WALKING, ON THE LEVEL – Norman Buckley (£6.95)

MOSTLY DOWNHILL: LEISURELY WALKS, LAKE DISTRICT – Alan Pears (£6.95)

100 LAKE DISTRICT HILL WALKS – Gordon Brown (£7.95)

PUB WALKS IN THE LAKE DISTRICT – Neil Coates (£6.95)

PUB WALKS IN THE YORKSHIRE DALES – Clive Price (£6.95)

PUB WALKS ON THE NORTH YORK MOORS & COAST – Stephen Rickerby (£6.95)

PUB WALKS IN THE YORKSHIRE WOLDS – Tony Whittaker (£6.95)

BEST PUB WALKS IN & AROUND SHEFFIELD – Clive Price (£6.95)

SOUTH YORKSHIRE WALKS – Martin Smith (£6.95)

YORKSHIRE DALES WALKING: ON THE LEVEL – Norman Buckley *(£6.95)*

MOSTLY DOWNHILL IN THE PEAK DISTRICT – Clive Price *(£6.95)*
(two volumes, White Peak & Dark Peak)

DISCOVERY WALKS IN DERBYSHIRE - Paul & Sandra Biggs *(£6.95)*

EAST CHESHIRE WALKS – Graham Beech *(£6.95)*

WEST CHESHIRE WALKS – Jen Darling *(£5.95)*

WALKS IN MYSTERIOUS WALES – Laurence Main *(£6.95)*

PUB WALKS IN SNOWDONIA – Laurence Main *(£6.95)*

RAMBLES AROUND MANCHESTER – Mike Cresswell *(£5.95)*

WEST PENNINE WALKS – Mike Cresswell *(£5.95)*

All Sigma books are available from bookshops. In case of difficulty, or for a free catalogue, contact:
Sigma Leisure, 1 South Oak Lane, Wilmslow, Cheshire SK9 6AR.
Phone: 01625 – 531035   Fax: 01625 – 536800.
ACCESS and VISA orders welcome. Please add £2 p&p to all orders.

 MAGAZINE

 EVENTS

 COMPETITIONS

 MEMBER DISCOUNTS

 TASTINGS & SAMPLING

 A FREE GIFT WHEN YOU JOIN

Tea is our most social and sociable drink – a part of our national heritage and daily life for well over 300 years. The Tea Club exists so its members can share and enjoy the history, traditions and romance associated with this fascinating drink.

THERE'S SO MUCH MORE
TO TEA THAN JUST
A CUPPA !

HOW TO JOIN

Simply send your name, full address and postcode to:

The Tea Club

PO Box 221

Guildford, Surrey GU1 3YT

and an application form will be sent to you immediately.

Tea Club Memberships are also a great gift idea – why not send one to a friend !